'Nikolas Badminton cracks the code on the leadership model for the future in this must-read masterpiece.'

Josh Linkner, five-time tech entrepreneur, *New York Times* bestselling author, venture capital investor

'In this increasingly volatile and uncertain world it's even more important to be prepared and build resilience in your business through proven methods well explained by Nikolas Badminton.'

Paul Polman, Co-founder and Chair of IMAGINE, former CEO of Unilever

'Whether you are a CEO of an organisation that is in transition, or a pioneer that is looking for new ways of looking at the future, this book will give you extensive knowledge and practical tools… A must read for every new or experienced futurist!'

Loes Damhof, UNESCO Chair in Futures Literacy

'Nikolas provides important thinking on exploring realistic and holistic futures that support planning for a resilient human race.'

Youssef Nassef, Climate Adaptation Director, United Nations (UNFCCC)

'Frank, succinct, and fundamentally optimistic, just like Nikolas himself, *Facing Our Futures* is the manual you need to make sense of, and more importantly, be a part of creating the sorts of collaborative, inspiring, sustainable futures we all want to arrive at.'

Bronwyn Williams, Futurist & Partner at Flux Trends

'There's no doubt that holistic futures design is the missing link for disruptive thinkers. You have to read this book and see how Nikolas takes world leading companies to the next level!'

Shawn Kanungo, Disruption Strategist, speaker and author of *The Bold Ones*

'Nikolas supplies the framework to upgrade your strategic planning capabilities and establish futures consciousness in your organization.'

Tom Goodwin, Innovation Leader and author of *Digital Darwinism*

'*Facing Our Futures* is an erudite and practical framework through which businesses can analyze a wide range of future outcomes, and then develop strategies that enable them to outflank the competition over years or even decades.'

David Rodnitzky, Founder, 3Q/DEPT

'An incredibly thoughtful work, pulling insightful resources from diverse fields, written in a skeptic, pragmatic and relevant manner, [which] seeks to discover more truths as data comes in. Very addictive and quenching.'

Saško Despotovski, Managing Director, Hinna Park Capital

Facing Our Futures

HOW FORESIGHT, FUTURES DESIGN AND STRATEGY CREATES PROSPERITY AND GROWTH

Nikolas Badminton

BLOOMSBURY BUSINESS
LONDON • OXFORD • NEW YORK • NEW DELHI • SYDNEY

BLOOMSBURY BUSINESS
Bloomsbury Publishing Plc
50 Bedford Square, London, WC1B 3DP, UK
29 Earlsfort Terrace, Dublin 2, Ireland

BLOOMSBURY, BLOOMSBURY BUSINESS and the Diana logo are trademarks of Bloomsbury Publishing Plc

First published in Great Britain 2023

A catalogue record for this book is available from the British Library

Library of Congress Cataloguing-in-Publication data has been applied for

ISBN: 978-1-3994-0023-7; eBook: 978-1-3994-0024-4

2 4 6 8 10 9 7 5 3 1

Typeset by Deanta Global Publishing Services, Chennai, India
Printed and bound in Great Britain by CPI Group (UK) Ltd, Croydon CR0 4YY

For Maximilian – be curious, brave and have hope as you look towards our futures

Contents

Acknowledgements

My partner Sarah and my son Maximilian – thank you for the support, inspiration and patience. My mother Carol and dad Roger. Nancy. Gary and Catherine. Kharis and Jane O'Connell, Ryan and Rachel Betts, Nick Black, Andrew Howell and Meena Sandhu, Andrew Jackson – the OG DARK FUTURES crew. The Pirates. Gila Golub and her community, especially Mary Ealden for the constant support. Tiffany Hamilton and John Bruce. Joel and Tasha Greensite. Yousef Nassef and the team at UNFCCC. Billie and Marc Carn. Dré Labre. Leah Zaidi. Matt Nelson. Sarah Tesla, Polina Bachlakova and Amber Case for believing in my first futures event. Landon Gunn. Jordan Eshpeter. Chris Dancy. Mike Merrill. Carl Schmidt and the UNBOUNCE crew. JP Holecka, Dave Smith. Josh Ingelby. Qasim Virjee and the Startwell crew. Rafeeq Bosch. Saško Despotovski. Glen Hiemstra, Dr. Cindy Frewen, Richard Yonck, Anne Boysen, Ramez Naam. Jared Nichols. Melissa Eshaghbeigi. Karl Schroeder. Dr. Jake Sotiriadis. Dr. Wendy Schultz. Dr. Joseph Voros. Madeline Ashby. Brett Macfarlane. Tracey Follows. Theo Priestly. Bronwyn Williams. Oksana Andreiuk. Liza Amlani. Loes Damhof. Ian Burbidge. Carol Ann Hilton. Pia Puolakka. Rotem Petranker. Phil Batalgas. Dana Martens. Peter Nowak. Natalie Nixon. Rocky Ozaki. Monika Bielskyte. Cathy Hackl. Ben Feist. Marianne Lefever. Shawn Kanungo. Denny Unger. Denise Brennan. Samantha Mathews. Sarah Prevette. Keith Ippel. Katie Metaverse. John Gray. Freddie and Karen Ghatala. Amanda Klassen. Bernd Patek. Eric Termuende. Jeremy Shaki. Norman Armour. Kristy O'Leary. Natalie Godfrey. LaSandra Hunt. Michelle Sklar. Karen Geary. Jen Browne. Megan Brand. Trish Neufeld. Ann Shin and the Fathom Film crew. Nikola Danaylov. Drex. Lynda Steele. Jeff Sammut. Michael Hiscock and the CTV Your Morning crew. Cory Ashworth and Janice Ungaro. Ryan Semeniuk. Catherine Roy. Petek Unsal. Jeff Jacobsen. All my speaker agency friends in Canada, UK and the United States. Josh Linkner and the 3 Ring Circus/Impact Eleven crew. All the speakers at From Now, Future Camp and DARK FUTURES. All the clients that have inspired me to push further and take bigger chances. The Royal Society for the Encouragement of Arts, Manufactures and Commerce (RSA). A huge shout out to so many people who have been great to virtually discuss this book and the field of futures design and foresight across social media. Also, a big thanks to Joe Wallace, Laura James and the folks at the Coachella Valley Economic Partnership (CVEP) that gave me a space to write this book during my retreat in Palm Desert.

Most importantly, the Agua Caliente Band of Cahuilla Indians, the hən̓q̓əmin̓əm̓- and skqxwu7mesh-speaking peoples, the Musqueam, Squamish, and Tsleil-Waututh Nations, the Mississaugas of the Credit, the Anishnabeg, the Chippewa, the Haudenosaunee and the Wendat peoples and all Naïve American, First Nations, Inuit and Métis peoples. I pay tribute to these and the indigenous peoples of the world. We truly owe a great debt to you, and we must listen to and learn from you more than we do each day.

Foreword by Glen Hiemstra

The human species has a remarkable ability to remember and learn from the past, to dream about, anticipate and envision the future, and to live in and devise immediate actions in the present. While we may not be as unique in these abilities when compared to other species as we once thought, still it is a shame to note how little we humans – whether as a species, as communities, as organizations, as individuals – engage these skills to create the potential for better futures. It is a strange paradox that we can remember and anticipate and dream, but most of our behaviour in the present seems designed to merely muddle through without ever looking back or ahead.

The modern practice of *futures studies*, begun around 1970 or so and now more commonly labelled *strategic foresight*, has been an effort to remedy this paradox. This new book by Nikolas Badminton is a contribution to the literature of both why the project of strategic foresight is worthwhile and how to go about doing it in systematic and effective ways.

My own journey into becoming a professional futurist began with exposure to the works of Dr Ed Lindaman, Fred Polak and Alvin Toffler as the 1970s began, then later the works of Barbara Marx Hubbard, Hazel Henderson, Elise Boulding and many others. Of the original three only Toffler is particularly well known. More about him in a moment. Lindaman, a college president when I met him, had been director of program planning for the Apollo project at North American Rockwell, and was a philosophical thinker about the very long-term future. He crystallized three fundamental questions about the future – what is probable, what is possible and what is preferred, arguing that exploration of the first two questions provides the best raw material with which to answer the third and ultimate question – what future do we want, and by extension which steps might we take that make preferred futures more likely? Lindaman was an ardent student of Pierre Teilhard de Chardin, the French theologian, scientist and philosopher. Chardin once famously wrote:

'One could say that the whole of life lies in seeing – if not ultimately, at least essentially. To be more is to be more united – and this sums up and is the very conclusion of the work to follow. But unity grows, and we will affirm this again, only if it is supported by an increase of consciousness, of vision. That is probably why the history of the living world can be reduced to the elaboration of ever more perfect eyes at the heart of a cosmos where it is always possible to discern more.'[1]

Enhancing our ability to 'see' is in many ways at the heart of strategic foresight, not in the sense of seeing precisely what is to happen in the future but in the sense of enlarging our understanding of possibilities, of future options, and thus finally of our own role in creating and not merely responding to the future.

Not long after I met Dr Lindaman, *The Image of the Future*, the seminal study by Dutch sociologist and futurist Fred Polak, was published in English.[2] The 1973 translation of Polak's original work, by Elise Boulding, is still typically listed among the foundational works of futures studies. Polak 'was the first in the post-World War II period to undertake the difficult conceptual work of clarifying the role of the image of the future in the social process at the societal level' (preface to *The Image of the Future*, 1973, p. vii).

Focused on the history of Western cultures, and thus subject to contemporary post-colonial futurist critiques, Polak nevertheless laid out the provocative thesis which became a cornerstone of my own futurist writing and consulting. He wrote:

[1] Sarah Appleton-Weber, 'The Human Phenomenon', 2003

[2] Fred L. Polak and Elise Boulding, 'The Image of the Future', 1962, *Journal of Political Economy*

> 'Any student of the rise and fall of cultures cannot fail to be impressed by the role played in this historical succession by the image of the future. The rise and fall of images precedes or accompanies the rise and fall of cultures. As long as a society's image is positive and flourishing, the flower of culture is in full bloom. Once the image begins to decay and lose its vitality, however, the culture does not long survive.' (*The Image of the Future*, p. 19)

In her preface, Elise Boulding commented: 'The pessimistic tone of the second part of *The Image of the Future*, as Polak depicts moment-ridden man trapped in a moment-bound culture, never gives way to despair. At every turn, the author reminds us that there still is a turning possible, that new vistas can open up'.

Here again we see a call for new ways of seeing, for new vistas that can enable us to escape the trap of a 'moment-bound' culture. It has been this fundamental viewpoint that led me to conclude that the most potent leverage point for change in communities and organizations is indeed the image of the future. If, by doing the work of strategic foresight, or futuring, people change what they expect to happen or think is possible in the future, or change their vision of preferred futures, then they feel driven to reconsider their present plans and actions. In other words, change the future and the present will follow.

Of course, it was Alvin Toffler, working with his spouse Heidi, who captured the anxiety of those trapped in a moment-bound culture but confronted with rapid and unrelenting change, in his best seller *Future Shock* in 1970. For me, a college student at the time, this book challenged my concepts about change and stability.

A decade later, I met Toffler at a gathering of the original World Future Society, where he asked in his keynote why the field of futures studies, then more than a decade old, had had so little apparent impact on public policy. His own answer was that the field to that point had focused too much on identifying likely futures, and not enough on exploring less likely but highly impactful possible futures.

Which brings us back to Nikolas Badminton and his current book. The unusual contribution that Nikolas has been bringing to the field of strategic foresight is his insistence on including what he calls 'dark futures' in the discussion of future images, and doing so with a very long view, as in hundreds or even thousands of years rather than the quite short time horizons that most futurists adopt.

As the first quarter of the twenty-first century draws towards a close, it is quite clear that possible dystopias loom. In my reading, Nikolas' thesis is that only by anticipating possible dystopias and confronting the meaning of them, as a part of strategic foresight, can we gain the courage and motivation to choose something better. Indeed, in my experience while the image of the future is a key leverage point for change, it is only a sense of urgency that gets people to begin to move out of our moment-bound existence. We hope, and we move, only if we see.

Glen Hiemstra
Futurist Emeritus at futurist.com
and founder of the Futurist Think Tank

Preface: Priming Futures Thinking

A personal journey to enlightenment, and progressive futures design practices.

It was late September in 2016. Autumn was in the air. I stood at the north-west corner of Georgia Street and Granville Street in Vancouver, British Columbia – a city I had transplanted myself to some eight years earlier.

I stopped and felt very aware of the world around me. I looked up from my smartphone and across the urban landscape. I could feel the pulse of the city – the complex interaction of people and transportation systems – and sense the tech infrastructure surrounding me. I felt like Neo when he woke from being shot by Agent Smith to see the Matrix at the end of the first of that trilogy of films.

While there were no falling codes, agents or women in red in sight, I was wildly aware of the obvious and hidden systems. In fact, metaphorically these *were* systems built from code and electric pulses. At that moment I remember wondering how I got to that point of view, and that level of perception.

Throughout my life I have developed an awareness that allows me to unconsciously see patterns and leads me to overanalyze the world around me. This has led to a futures consciousness that I continually review and develop as I gather more signals and identify trends. In addition to this I more easily imagine the negative situations that result from our actions today. To be honest, I've thought like that for most of my 50 years.

Today, I'm a dreamer, futurist, a foresight practitioner and a *hope engineer* – another term I interlace with *futurist*. I'm also a new father – that sure flips your thinking on its head. I love life. I love the world. I am also deeply concerned about what may play out as we career towards our futures.

What was once a hindrance – the trait of seeing both positive and dystopian futures – has led me to a practice of continual reflection, and a modus operandi of honest and direct conversations and communication. That has led me to build a collective of great thinkers – the Futurist Think Tank – and to build teams of people to work with clients to explore equitable, sustainable and responsible futures. The clients we work with just happen to be some of the biggest and most impactful companies and governments in the world – and some are start-ups looking to disrupt those very organizations.

My workdays – which these days are most days – are challenging, creative and exciting. I've also realized that it is really tough to live with what I call the *burden of foresight*, the wild awareness. I guess it is a superpower.

This book is a culmination of my life and professional experiences in considering what our futures may be. I've stumbled from business and technology strategy into futures design and foresight, and over time have developed a point of view and a set of methods that I will share in this book.

The work I do with my team and clients is about suspending our beliefs of how we imagine the future to be, and to open our eyes and minds to the possibilities for many futures and new ways of operating in the world together in order to address the biggest challenges we face. A key part of this is to consider positive and dystopian trajectories and futures to create a worldview without censoring possibilities of what may go wrong – something that's prevalent in the narratives and storytelling in modern society.

My life has been interesting and continues to inform the work we do.

Becoming a Futurist

I was born in 1972 in the United Kingdom. The 1970s and '80s were strange times, ruled by complexity wrought by our unchecked industrial complex, short-term thinking, and political wrangling with what seemed like little consideration for humanity or our preserved futures.

Between the ages of eight and nine, two pivotal things happened in my life.

The first was that I was bought a book about the year 2000 and beyond – *The Usborne Book of the Future.* It was a mind-expanding, technological trip through time to the year 2000 and beyond. This was a child's book that speculated on what the 2000s were going to be like. Some of the predictions are remarkably close to things we have now, and others are not. All of them were about a single, modular future with hyperloops, moon colonies, wrist computers and so much more. I loved the suspension of disbelief and view of the future.

The second pivotal moment for me was the first time I used a home computer. It was a British Broadcasting Corporation Microcomputer System, also known as a BBC Micro. My cousin had one and we'd link it to the small portable TV in his room, and then he'd show me how to upload games like Manic Miner and play. This was a magical and definitive moment. Having a computer became an absolute must-have in my life. Eventually, a couple of years later, my folks would buy me a Sinclair ZX Spectrum – huge respect to the now deceased Sir Clive Sinclair, who I feel did more for computer literacy in the UK in the 1980s than anyone else.

During the 1980s the world was going through a step change towards being data-driven and tech-centric. At the same time, I embraced the burgeoning subculture of punk rock, skateboarding, exploration of new ideas in media and design, and class rebellion. At the same time, I dived in deeper and deeper while spending countless hours hidden in public libraries reading encyclopedias and thumbing through books on Eastern religions and strategic thinking – *The Tibetan Book of the Dead*, Sun Tzu's *The Art of War*, and the *The Book of Five Rings* written by the legendary, innovative and deeply philosophical Japanese swordsman Miyamoto Musashi.

It was at that time I found George Orwell. I devoured *Animal Farm* and *Nineteen Eighty-Four*. The vision of a future he truly believed might come to pass (*Nineteen Eighty-Four* more than *Animal Farm*, that is) presented a crumbling society with overarching control from Big Brother who perpetuated a corporatized authoritarian world defined by newspeak to diminish the range of thought – a hyper-aggressive Overton window,[3] and ultimately ruled by totalitarianism. I wondered why they didn't embrace such texts in the school curriculum over *Cider with Rosie*.

[3] 'What is the Overton window?', 2015, *New Statesman*

Orwell's imagined worlds felt far on the horizon and yet also familiar. It felt like he gave me permission to explore dystopian ideas of what the world may turn out to be in an unchecked, totalitarian state.

In 1993 I started studying Applied Psychology and Computing – cognitive psychology, computing, database design, human-computer interaction, complexity and chaos theory, linguistics and the early days of artificial intelligence. The professors seemed like misfits willing to embrace more edgy ideas on the futures that were likely to come with advancing the human-computer ecosystem.

When I started, I found the ability to use some of my outlying ideas of where we're likely headed. I embraced the cognitive and organizational psychology aspects and started to dig deeper into the emerging culture of the World Wide Web.

Around that time, I also read *Cyberia*, a book by Douglas Rushkoff which delved into early cyberpunk culture. Rushkoff describes his book as 'a very special moment in our recent history – a moment when anything seemed possible. When an entire subculture – like a kid at a rave trying virtual reality for the first time – saw the wild potentials of marrying the latest computer technologies with the most intimately held dreams and the most ancient spiritual truths.'[4]

I learned about the early days of Internet communities, the teachings of Terence McKenna and the pioneers of virtual reality (VR) like Jaron Lanier – two people I hold in very high regard to this day – and these changed how I considered our futures by introducing me to the spiritual side of technology.

It was an exciting time to be paying attention to the changing world, the signals of change, the emerging trends, and the promises of a new egalitarian future for all – connected by the World Wide Web.

I didn't know then that some 20 years later I would be speaking to audiences around the world about all these technologies and their potential for business, and also their limiting effects on society. It still excites me today.

---

[4] Douglas Rushkoff, 'Cyberia: Preface to the 1994 paperback edition', 2022

I have worked for tech companies and consultancies reimagining ways of working with and manipulating data: modelling of consumer behaviour through to behavioural targeting and profiling people for profit (how little did I realize the scale of what it would be today).

In 2008 I moved permanently to Canada. Vancouver seemed to have an exciting air about it. The West Coast libertarian values, pockets of anarchy and proximity to Seattle, Portland and San Francisco were great.

I shifted gears to work on defining progressive digital strategies and new frameworks for analytics and digital transformation for advertising agencies. I started to veer more into what was futures work at this time, even though I never called it that. I challenged clients to make brave steps to ensure resiliency and relevancy in the new world of social media, content and new forms of online community building.

In 2010 I reconnected with an old friend who had moved to Vancouver. Even though we had not spoken in person for 18 years it felt like just a few minutes had passed, and we were both deeply involved in tech, systems design, counterculture and shaking things up.

On a rainy November morning in 2012, that friend and I jumped in my car and drove eight hours down Highway 1 across the border into the United States to Portland. There was an event being hosted by the cyborg anthropologist Amber Case. She had delivered a breakthrough talk TEDWomen, called 'We're all cyborgs now', and was now organizing an *unconference* called Cyborg Camp. It was a compelling thing to consider our physical states merging with technology.

It was held in an office and accommodated a ragtag group of futures thinkers on how human–computer interaction was developing. Talks on the quantified self, synaesthesia through application and data layers, and turning yourself into the world's first publicly traded person (shout out to KmikeyM, who keeps going with that). After the event I approached Amber and said that I'd love to host the same event in Vancouver.

A few months later, on 11 May 2013, I hosted Cyborg Camp YVR with several keynote speakers, who uncovered everything from robotic surgery, wearable computing, liquid interfaces, historical applications of social media (design fiction), and the need to build a foundation of love when designing new systems of technology. One hundred and twenty-five people came from all over North America, a crowd that created incredible buzz and considerations of the opportunities and challenges we face in our technological world.

Later that year I was at a local event and a friend introduced me to a group of technology investors as a *futurist*. It was certainly unprompted and surprising to me. But as I thought about the remit of that role in the world, I felt excited yet uneasy. I also knew the discipline needed new thinking and drive, so I dived into understanding futures design and developed my persona in that field with a focus on our future lives impacted by exponential technologies.

The following year I ran a conference called From Now and worked with a product designer to build physical plinths and sculptures that brought our attendees' ideas of our futures together. That is what we now know as *speculative fiction*, a discipline that has gained pace and become important for organizations to consider.

I then went on to produce an event called Future Camp, another 'unconference' that aimed to bring people together to discuss and debate where our futures are taking us.

Then, on one sunny late September afternoon in 2014, I was having drinks with three friends and discussing the weird underbelly of our unequal and technical experience – sharks chewing on internet cables in Thailand, dark patterns in mobile design, and how our physical attributes betray our psychological intentions – the likelihood to be a liar, or even a murderer. That inspired me to create a new event called DARK FUTURES.

This was a conference that investigated the dark recesses of the systems surrounding us. DARK FUTURES persists as what some people call the 'Black Mirror of TED Talks', with events held each year in Toronto, Vancouver and San Francisco.

Based on the presentations that dozens of people have done at DARK FUTURES and other events, it has become normal over the years to look at the hidden systems, inconvenient truths and negative effects of the decisions made today which are meant to provide foundations for our collective futures. The short-term hopes that dissolve into dystopian society.

Over the past 10 years my futures practice has matured from being primarily around trends and technologies that impact human culture towards a larger worldview. It's become clear that a balanced humanistic approach is needed by all governments and companies because they have forgotten how important this world and the balance between humanity and nature truly is. My continual research and thinking considers positive possible futures and the uneven, unfair and dystopian futures as well. Something that few are willing to do publicly.

Facing Our Futures

The idea of framing our situations and feelings from a position of darkness and struggle is an important cultural and existential tool for governments, businesses and collaborators across the globe. We know those leaders and executives prefer to not see what could go wrong and hope that the path we find is good. If it's not, then the corporations that prescribed the systems to us quickly outsource the blame to us. They call this *experience* and *perspective* to deflect criticism.

My contribution to the futures design field thus far has been to realize that if we can open our eyes and embrace those dystopian futures that may lie ahead of us, we can create an advantage for ourselves via foresight.

I have further developed this ability to formulate an approach where my team and I work with executives and government leaders to use both positive and dystopian thinking to build optimism and resiliency through strengthened strategic planning, anticipated risk and developing bold visions of our collective futures.

My futures design practice is underpinned by constantly scanning for those signals – geopolitical, technological, societal and cultural – which indicate that change is coming. I also consider the structure and dynamics of positive futures by first considering the potential for dystopian futures.

I have collected these approaches in a proprietary framework – the Positive-Dystopia Framework – which allows for building provocative visions of our futures through the definition of principles, scanning for signals and developing hypothetical what-if scenarios. In addition is the visceral colour we can add to this through speculative fiction, experiential futures and storytelling.

My goal, and ongoing work, aims to help world leaders, governments and executives gain a broader perspective on the world and the possible futures, anticipate unforeseen risks, and (hopefully) stem future losses – human, natural and/or financial.

Now is the time for world leaders and the people shaping our world to understand there is no perfect future (singular), and that short-term thinking is both prevalent and dangerous. Blinkered and near-term goals have led humanity to question our ability to be resilient and accelerate our trajectory towards possible industrial and societal collapse. Short-term decisions that have framed the visions and solutions for us all have driven progress and profit at any cost, and today we find ourselves facing dystopian realities where decline and collapse is our roadmap.

I've written *Facing Our Futures* to provide an opportunity for executives, world leaders, policymakers, activists, designers, strategists and foresight practitioners to explore and create a broader perspective. In this book, I challenge the idea that we must solely plan for 'good', 'safer', or 'ideal' positive futures and develop a long-term view of our futures, and that we must embrace possible dystopian futures as well.

I discuss the industrial complex that has captured us, and how long-term thinking and the discipline of foresight can provide proactive anticipation of unforeseen risks and resilient strategic planning today. I also take you through the process of foresight I've used with clients and highlight essential thinking and best practices in the field – signal scanning, world-building, developing futures scenarios, producing speculative fiction and backcasting.

I detail the Positive-Dystopian Framework and take you through its method, exploring how it can be applied to help organizations and governments build more realistic, resilient and balanced pathways to our futures.

The ideas presented in this book are an invitation to broaden your horizons and consider integrating futures thinking into your strategic planning.

CHAPTER ONE

WHAT IS FORESIGHT?

The discipline of foresight is considerate, nuanced and deeply reflective. It's also been shaped by a deep exploration of what our futures could be.

By avoiding thinking about the future you hand over the future, as a prisoner, to the ... unthinking. Futures studies seek to subvert such status quo. They help to keep options open in an institutionally closed world.

Ashis Nandy

There it is: the future. Look at it. Glorious, pristine, accessible. Yours. Built by us. We are the people – the organization – that can corral investors and resources to make it happen. All you need to do is believe in what we do, and it's possible. With resolve and support we simply cannot fail, but it won't be easy. Yet, nothing is truly impossible. We just need to trust in science, technology and shooting for the moon. And we just need several billion dollars and a few years to make this future a reality.

Stop! There's a prevalence and a big problem with this narrative.

The billionaire technocrats, politicians and fervent investors are *not* looking out for us and our futures. They want to define a closed ecosystem and narrow view that can easily be regulated and policed by the terms and conditions we happily accept so that we are reduced to being *users*. It's the antithesis to how we as humans and our complex societal structures operate. These are often the same people who think that living to 120 years old, becoming a multi-planet species, and the exponential growth of technological solutions is a bigger goal than being a thriving and sustainable multi-species planet that carefully respects and considers the relationship between humanity, the natural world and our industrial complex.

I'll be honest. When I entered the world of foresight and began working as a futurist, I wholeheartedly leaned into the hyperbole of big tech predictions and similar promises. After several years at the frontline my heart has been somewhat broken, I tend now to veer towards discussions around equality and equity, challenging colonial thinking, and fighting against the rulers of our failing industrial complex. I also reflect on the power dynamics of our modern world, as I know these ideas on our collective future (singular) do not exist.

Equally, I know that unbridled positives and the heralded utopian futures are not coming – no matter what we do, or however much money we throw at it. The rhetoric of leaders has created a technophilic view that is ingrained into our young thinkers. In 1985, here's what Steve Jobs said in an interview that year:

> 'At Apple, people are putting in 18-hour days. We attract a different type of person – a person who doesn't want to wait five or 10 years to have someone take a giant risk on him or her. Someone who really wants to get in a little over his head and make a dent in the universe.'

Sure, Apple has made a 'dent in the universe' if you think that more sculpted iPhones, iPads, MacBook Pros, and subscription services are it. But these now essential devices will not save us from the futures ahead of us – they'll just allow us to take selfies and 4K slow motion videos of our plight on the burning platforms on which we are all standing on.

By now I get the feeling that you are gauging my tone. I am a sceptic, pragmatist and realist. I am also deeply hopeful about the collective human race and what we each can do to create amazing futures for all. We just need to broaden our minds, consider where we came from, gain a comprehensive understanding of where we are today (and the complex dynamics in play), and start to create pathways forward on multiple trajectories to see what good and challenging (some may say dystopian) futures are possible in 10, 20 or even 30+ years.

What is foresight, and why is it important?

Foresight is the practice of how we come together to think critically about our world and how our futures may play out. It's a creative discipline where we collect signals and great ideas to help us imagine scenarios that inch us towards a world where we can thrive. It's also about reflecting the histories that must be considered in the futures contexts that we are exploring.

Foresight is an essential discipline for any progressive executive and organization to build. In today's world strategy is short-sighted without foresight, and many organizations are stepping up to enhance their planning capabilities. With foresight, we are concerned with two things:

Longer-term horizons – futures that are usually at least 10 years away. My colleague Dr Cindy Frewen says that anything less than 10 years is *strategy* although there may be some exceptions to this, especially in its use in private business – we often see that in our work. I would argue that we need to push our thinking out to horizons of 10, 20, 50 and 100+ years. The further we look, the more fantastical and freer our futures become, and a number of areas comfortably live in these times – urban design, power station construction or other major infrastructural decisions around the water-food-energy-waste nexus.

Alternative futures – it is helpful to examine alternative paths of development, not just what is currently believed to be most likely or business as usual. Often foresight will construct multiple scenarios. These may be an interim step on the way to creating what may be known as positive visions, success scenarios, aspirational futures. They also allow us to see the challenges and risks. Sometimes alternative scenarios will be a major part of the output of foresight work, with the decision about what future to build being left to other mechanisms.

These two considerations are fundamental. However, foresight must also be seen as a reality check that includes the ideas of both dystopian and positive futures that can actively influence organizational strategy, public policy, research and cultural development. This dichotomy has informed my work, as well as the methods and discussions included in this book.

It's important that we don't consider foresight to be a side-of-the-table task, whimsical value system or philosophical stance within an organization. Instead, see it as an evolving set of core organizational competencies in which we invest, develop, nurture and share openly over time.

In modern organizations the real challenge is that strategic planning is typically restricted to the next 12 months or a cycle of 3 or 4 years that is monitored by executives focused on key performance indicators. Our modern world is a place where CEOs and executives are rewarded for short-term achievements, and we have politicians purely thinking in election cycles. The two are generally linked societally by aspiration, partnership and lobbying. Ultimately, this has left us with a lack of responsibility, accountability and vision of what our futures need to be for humanity to thrive.

It's time for executives, world leaders, and people shaping a path for our world to understand there is no perfect positive future (singular), and our short-term thinking is endemic and dangerous.

It's time to embrace foresight as a discipline that empowers us to look at horizons that lie beyond our short-term cycles of strategic planning – 10, 20, 30, and even 100+ years. To create long-term resiliency by considering our decisions and actions today.

A brief history of foresight

I came to foresight, and futures design, as a formal discipline a little later in my career through curiosity, exploration and a little serendipity. I wholeheartedly stepped into this new discipline and challenged my ideas on the futures that may lie ahead of us. The foresight folks out in the world – from business, philanthropy, research and development (R & D) and academia – have really impressed me in their discipline and application of methods to imagine resilient futures. Foresight is a unique discipline where so many different people can come together from so many backgrounds and have an impact on how we collectively think about our futures and then make plans to address the challenges in the world today.

I'm going to provide several interesting reference points on the development of foresight as a discipline. I am also going to lean on some great thinkers in the field and their perspectives.

The discipline of foresight is not new and its history goes back thousands of years. I'll not aim to detail all of that here and you can see Marek Jemala's paper from 2009, 'Evolution of foresight in the global historical content',[5] to see when and where key moments,

[5] Marek Jemala, 'Evolution of foresight in the global historical context', 2009, Emerald Group Publishing

historical events and inventions contributed to the modern discipline of foresight.

I'll start a little closer to where we are today – on 19 November, 1932. That evening the BBC[6] presented a talk by notable science fiction author H. G. Wells in which he called for the appointment of *Professors of Foresight* to explore the implications of the development of new inventions and devices:

> 'It seems an odd thing to me that though we have thousands and thousands of professors and hundreds of thousands of students of history working upon the records of the past, there is not a single person anywhere who makes a whole-time job of estimating the future consequences of new inventions and new devices. There is not a single Professor of Foresight in the world. But why shouldn't there be? All these new things, these new inventions, and new powers, come crowding along; every one is fraught with consequences, and yet it is only after something has hit us hard that we set about dealing with it.'

Wells chose as an example the rapid spread of the motor car, which had serious consequences for modern life and took society by surprise. He suggested that an educational institution replete with a faculty of professors, who can prepare us for the changes wrought by advances in technology, will deliver foresight for modern society.

Over time many universities stepped up to create significant faculties and courses that deliver qualifications in foresight: Stellenbosch in South Africa, the University of Houston and University of Hawai'i

[6] 'Communications 1922–1932 – HG Wells', BBC Archive and originally broadcast on 19 Nov 1932, 21:50 on National Programme Daventry

at Mānoa in the United States, Ontario College of Art & Design (OCAD) University in Canada, Swinburne University of Technology in Australia, and many others. These are bolstered by many organizations providing training and consultancy as well, much like the Futurist Think Tank I run at futurist.com.

We're also seeing many futurists and foresight practitioners emerging within companies, creative and general interest groups that are less academic yet still speculative and interested in ideas for the futures in which their organizations want to play a part.

Futures Studies

In 1971 the Hawaii Research Center for Futures Studies was established by the Hawaii State Legislature. It's located within the Department of Political Science, College of Social Sciences at the University of Hawai'i at Mānoa and has established itself as one of the world's most renowned institutions to attend to learn about futures research, consulting and education. It has been instrumental in educating four decades of foresight practitioners and bringing foresight and futures thinking to governments, organizations, agencies and businesses around the world.

The Center was overseen by James Dator, who served as Secretary General and then President of the World Futures Studies Federation for a decade and produced numerous publications on futures studies and emergent issues. In 1979, he published a model of social change stories in the journal *Perspectives on Cross-Cultural Psychology* which defined four future perspectives. He revisited this model in his 2002 book *Advancing Futures* and further observed that all our narratives (signals-to-trends, stories, scenarios) on social change issues can be classified into four recurring groups of images, stories or policies regarding the effects of that change:

1) **Continuation** – the initial phase of slow growth, business as usual, more of the status quo, linear (expected) growth, or fast exponential growth that leads to a plateau.
2) **Limits and discipline** – behaviours to adapt to growing internal or environmental limits which can also be considered as the saturation phase of S-curve growth.
3) **Decline and collapse** – system degradation or failure modes as a crisis emerges, is resolved or exacerbated across its interdependent points.
4) **Transformation** – new technology, business, behaviours or social and cultural factors that change the game.

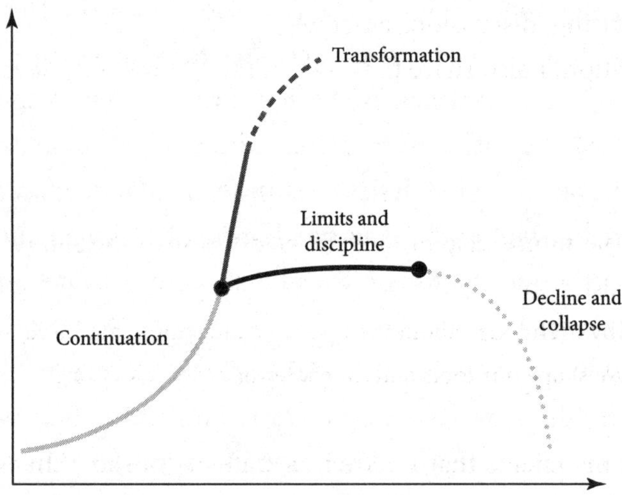

Fig 1.1 Dator's Four Futures

One major consideration for foresight practitioners is to recognize that all four futures have stories often told by different parties at the same time. These stories can be independent of each other and their interplay complex. If you were to dig into each futures state, and then across them, you can see the linkages and reference points across them and create richer perspectives within each.

I often use Dator's Four Futures model for framing the work that we do with clients because these simplistic ideas are typically understood by all – transformation is good, limits that lead into decline and collapse are bad. I also focus a significant amount of my time discussing decline and collapse as a catalyst for transformation and reinvention of purpose with clients. Especially in the application of the Positive-Dystopian Framework.

I relish the opportunity to sit down with a board of directors and ask: *What if the world no longer needs you, or sees you as relevant? What if the good times are over because you've been complacent for too long?* Then I sit back in silence to see what, usually uncomfortable and surprising, discussions emerge.

In addition, I also share the Laws of the Future[7] also developed by Dator:

1) 'The future' cannot be 'predicted' because 'the future' does not exist.
2) Any useful idea about the futures should appear to be ridiculous.
3) 'We shape our tools and thereafter our tools shape us.'[8]

I remind my clients that we are in a state of constant change where humanity, technology, industry and the natural world complexly

[7] Jim Dator, 'What futures studies is, and is not', 1995, Hawaii Research Center for Futures Studies

[8] This last point is attributed to Marshall McLuhan, the Canadian futurist and philosopher of media, and provides the starting point of a useful theory of social change.

interplay, thus creating ideas of possible futures that may be positive or dystopian.

The plurality of our futures

As we look beyond future states, we shift to the horizons ahead of us and the plurality in our futures. Another well-known foresight model helps us think about this – The Futures Cone, also called the Cone of Possibilities.

The Futures Cone was originally developed by Charles Taylor in 1991, with additional contributions in 1994 from Trevor Hancock and Clement Bezold. Later, in 2003, it was adapted and extended by the Australian futurist Dr Joseph Voros:

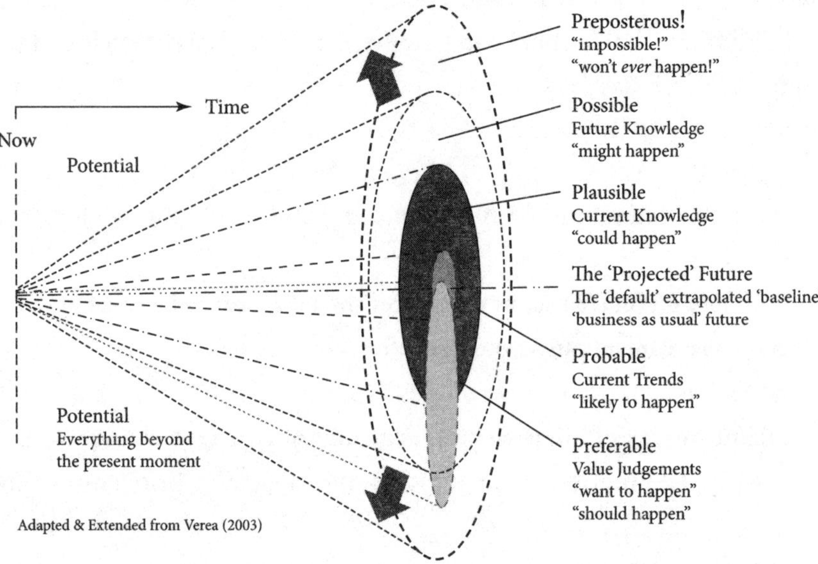

Fig. 1.2 The Futures Cone – Adapted and Extended from Voros 2017

This is an excellent way of thinking about and visualizing the futures ahead of us and it's referred to extensively in futures design.

The Futures Cone allows us to frame and set out a range of future scenarios, categorizing them into *projected*, *potential*, *possible*, *plausible*, *probable*, and *preferable* futures. Voros defines these six types of alternative futures and considers them to be explorations into ideas about the future that are based in the present moment and the signals that we see today:[9]

Projected – the (singular) default, business as usual, baseline, extrapolated 'continuation of the past through the present' future.
Potential – everything beyond the present moment is a potential future. This comes from the assumption that the future is undetermined and open, not inevitable or fixed, which is perhaps the foundational axiom of Futures Studies.
Possible – these are those futures that we think *might* happen, based on some future technology we do not yet possess, but which we might possess someday (e.g., warp drive).
Plausible – those we think *could* happen based on our current understanding of how the world works (physical laws, social processes etc).
Probable – those we think are *likely to* happen, usually based on (in many cases, quantitative) current trends.
Preferable – those we think *should* or *ought to* happen: normative value judgements as opposed to the mostly cognitive, above. There is also, of course, the associated converse class – the un-preferred futures – a *shadow* form of anti-normative futures that we think should not happen nor ever be allowed to happen (global climate change scenarios are an example that comes to mind).

[9] thevoroscope.com/2017/02/24/the-futures-cone-use-and-history/

Often it's easier to explore *possible*, *probable* and *preferable* futures in our work. They may not appear to be inherently dystopian, but once we see what more positive futures can be, we can then develop ideas of what *preposterous* futures could exist – both good and bad – and start to identify and amplify negative outcomes. That's a seventh type of alternative futures and likely the most potent for creating reaction and thought – Preposterous Futures.

In our modern age of disruption, we cannot say that something is truly impossible or won't ever happen. People have always vigorously argued against preposterous futures. Horses will never be replaced by cars. Humans will never fly. We will never land on the Moon. We will never clone humans. We will never time travel or teleport. OK, the last seems preposterous, but the world of quantum physics has started to open those possibilities up to us. (Currently there are a number of scientific and academic experiments investigating quantum time travel and teleportation.)

Over the years, I have often found myself discussing and playing with the ideas of preposterous futures in my career, through my writing and at the DARK FUTURES events. Preposterous futures allows us to see the 'ridiculous', 'impossible', or 'never going to happen' events, immersing our thoughts in a terrible future that might be wrought on us. There's nothing more alive and chaotic than a mind, government or organization thrust into survival mode, and it leads us down one of two paths: panic, or to mobilize strategic thinking and recognize mitigation plans against foreseen risks. That's where the value of exploring dystopias start to make sense.

I had the pleasure of chatting with Dr Voros in 2021 about his career and the Futures Cone. I wanted to ask him about the addition of Preposterous Futures:

'The idea of Preposterous Futures came when people were unwilling to admit to the idea that these things might happen, and because I was looking for a "P" I was digging through my old presentation slides and it became clear to me that I needed some way of moving beyond that, you know. Why is it that some people just stomp their feet and say, "No, that's impossible"? So, it's impossible it will happen, as opposed to possible it might happen.

'Right. Now, of course, most futurists that I know of, at least read some science fiction and are growing up with that. Arthur C. Clarke has his famous book *Profiles of the Future*,[10] that talks about failures of imagination and failures of nerve. There is this idea that failure of imagination means that you can't even conceive of it, you won't allow it. And that combines with Jim Dator's famous maxim.

'Clarke's second law is the way you find the limits of the possible is going beyond them into the impossible. Yeah. That leads to the idea that all the futures are impossible, they can't be possible. And that combines with Dator's, the second law of the future. So, there's two second laws there. Which is that any truly useful idea about the future should appear to be ridiculous.'

Another colleague and inspiration is Loes Damhof from the Hanze University of Applied Sciences in the Netherlands. I had the pleasure of working with her on the Resilience Frontiers Program for the United Nations and I chatted with her later as part of my Exponential Minds podcast. She laid down some wisdom about the

[10] Tim Radford, 'Profiles of the Future by Arthur C Clarke – review', 2011, *The Guardian*

real challenge when trying to let go of our reality and consider the futures ahead of us:

> 'If we let go of the notion that there's only one future, if we really want to make use of the full complexity of the universe and really want to embrace uncertainty, I think it's important that we diversify futures. And to do that, we need to stretch our cognitive flexibility to imagine both if you need different perspectives. And just to understand that there's not just one future in order to overcome what we call the poverty of imagination. If we're just letting one perspective determine the horizon as the future, then we're going to end up making the same mistakes in the past. So, we need to put different dots on the horizon, and we need to open up that horizon wider.'

I speak to clients about our collective *poverty of imagination*, and it seems to resonate and result in self-reflection and how to address it. The truth is that we have forgotten what it is like to daydream and work the metaphysical muscle that is our imagination while weighed down by social media, bills to pay, vacations to plan, kids to raise, fitness to maintain, which relationships to nurture and which to discard.

Yet, in modern business we have a deeply ingrained problem:

> Organizations actively kill imagination.

If you've reacted viscerally to that, then ask yourself why. And consider whether you really give the people you work with full rein in their roles to be creative and have time to daydream about the world at large and bring in new ideas. Also think about how you give new ideas the oxygen to breathe alongside the prioritized work in the organization.

Reigniting our imaginations and giving ourselves space to breath and move is as important to the discipline of foresight as any of the frameworks we use. Reigniting our curiosity, activating social dreaming and encouraging everyone to be open with their thoughts and feelings on multiple futures is essential.

People can become more skilled at *using the future* through collaboration. As humans we can tap into collective wisdom to be inspired and ignite our imaginations daily. Organizations have struggled to understand the value of exercising out imaginations; however, we are moving from an anecdotal state of how it helps to one where we know foresight and futures design adds incredible value.

What's the value of Corporate Foresight?

It wasn't until recently that a quantified value of foresight, from an organizational perspective, was explored in more detail. In 2018, René Rohrbeck and Menes Etingue Kum published their paper 'Corporate foresight and its impact on firm performance: A longitudinal analysis'.[11]

The researchers 'developed a model that judges a firm's future preparedness (FP) by assessing the need for corporate foresight and comparing it to the maturity of its corporate foresight practices. They measured future preparedness across several companies in 2008 and then its impact on their performance in 2015.'

Their study looked at several companies that have been undertaking corporate foresight as a core capability, including Cisco, Daimler, Deutsche Bank, Deutsche Telekom, France Telecom, L'Oréal, Pepsi,

---

[11] René Rohrbeck, Menes Etingue Kum, 'Corporate foresight and its impact on firm performance: A longitudinal analysis', 2018, *Technological Forecasting and Social Change*

Siemens and the Société Nationale des Chemins de Fer Français (SNCF). What they found was that only one in five organizations strategically prepares itself for future movements in their industries and associated markets – and just one in twenty organizations adjusts their course of action or strategic plans accordingly.

To undertake the study Rohrbeck and Kum divided the companies into four categories according to the challenges on the markets in which they operate.

1) **Vigilant** companies that work determinedly with corporate foresight in their market.
2) **Neurotic** companies that might adapt their course of action to the movements in the market but do so without a long-term or strategic perspective.
3) **Vulnerable** companies that have strategies, but whose strategies do not sufficiently address the challenges of their market.
4) **Companies in danger** that might have strategies, but whose strategies are completely insufficient.

After seven years each company's maturity was measured. It was found that the profitability of the neurotic and vulnerable companies was 37 per cent lower on average compared to the vigilant companies, while the companies in danger were lagging the vigilant by 44 per cent.

This powerful insight should awaken any executive to the need to be ready for the unknown futures ahead of us and invest in establishing foresight and futures design in their organization. I speculate that this study reveals how corporate foresight was making a big difference not only to company performance but to the overall culture and philosophical resolve of the companies themselves – as, indeed, the researchers noticed:

> 'Companies that recognize that the future might change the very foundation of their business, that prepare for it and change their course of action accordingly, are 33 per cent more profitable than companies on average. In addition, these vigilant companies have achieved a 200 per cent higher growth rate than the average company.'

Finally, something that executives and government leaders can identify with – profit and growth. I hope in our futures we can move beyond these two as wholly compelling, but this is a great start.

Over the past few years I've shared this quote and paper many times. It often prompts a discussion around the sample size of the study and thus the validity of these claims. Even so, I truly believe that it has helped shift thinking towards developing corporate foresight capabilities for many companies.

The role and mindset of a futurist

Futurists and Foresight Practitioners are relatively new players and influencers in the business world. There are six core areas of work that we undertake:

1) **Signal scanning** – we look for distinct pieces of information, statistics, stories, activities and/or events that indicate an impending change or emerging issue may become significant in the future. The strength of signals are determined through research and observing the amount of R & D activity, practical and useful ideas that solve real-world problems, levels of continued investment and predicted growth – in terms of US$ + Compound Annual Growth Rate (CAGR) figures. Media coverage also plays a part, though the media has a bad track record in terms of foresight and prefers catchy headlines and clickbait

– which is not all that useful in this process. Signals are the most useful when they are weak – i.e. in early stages but show incredible promise. They are speculative and experimental by nature. There's also a high chance that many of these solutions proposed will not come to fruition. However, we know that from a sea of ideas some world-changing ideas emerge as we investigate and connect the dots.

2) **Trend identification** – from the signals we identify trends. These are the general directions in which our world is developing or changing. They inherently have momentum and are created by existing conditions and environments. They are part of the reshaping of how we see the world and/or how we operate within it.
3) **Scenario building** – the signals and trends give us the reference points for what might come next, and scenarios explore how people will be affected. Building multiple scenarios with many, varied groups of people from differing backgrounds and demographics (age, gender, sexuality etc.) is so important. It's then we can see a bounty of great ideas, and equally, the gaps that we need to fill to ensure we cover a decent amount of ground on which to base our speculations.
4) **Speculative fiction and experiential futures** – beyond scenarios, we can travel down the rabbit hole into more emotional and visceral explorations of our futures through fiction, filmmaking, the creation of media and art. Speculative fiction and experiential futures are an invitation to experience the feelings, smells and shapes of our futures. For me, this is one of the most exciting and useful parts of foresight work. (We will explore this in further detail in Chapter 7: Igniting Imagination.)
5) **Linking out futures to our world today** – is not easy, and involves taking abstract and speculative ideas of what our futures may be in 10, 20, and even 50+ years. These then ignite action to take today to track and prepare for them, even though they may not come to pass as envisaged.

6) **Sense-making and seeking knowledge** – we read a lot of papers, online articles, books, have long text debates with friends, interview folks for podcasts, and follow the wise meanderings of many friends on social media. I often share new ideas in order to see the reaction of people I respect in the field. Each keynote speech I deliver to clients has a new idea in there, enabling me to gauge if it resonates and reflects off other more established ideas to lead to new thoughts and lines of inquiry.

If you summarize the intent behind these six areas above, you could say that we are travellers to our futures and oracles of what might pass. Spirit guides in a way. Cartographers of today, knowing both that there is much to be mapped ahead of us and that at this moment we can only wonder and wander in directions that 'feel right'.

No matter what, undertaking foresight is deeply satisfying work.

For many, the role of a futurist, or foresight practitioner, is like that of a super-creative professional who develops a style and never stops evolving, rather than a finite and regulated discipline of a business administrator, say, or a Chief Financial Officer, accountant or lawyer.

Ultimately foresight is an artisanal craft. Instead of baking a myriad of delicious pastries, we cook up a smorgasbord of fantastical futures quite unlike our current creations. Having said that, there are as many kinds of futurists as there are ways of thinking about the future.

We have to step up to be as radically imaginative, critical, inclusive and democratic as possible. It's OK to rustle some feathers and to be provocative. In fact, it's our duty. At the same time we must actively save words like *future* and *futurist* from the pop futurist and media hijackers who choose to abuse the terms and colonize the general public's perception of the stories of our futures: 'The future is crypto . . .' 'Artificial Intelligence and robotics will render us useless . . .' etc.,

etc. We must create our narratives together. They give us a better ability to build bigger visions, anticipate risks and strengthen strategic planning today.

When assuming the role of futurist – whether that is an extension of your current job, or a focus of your work – and thinking about rules for engagement, I encourage clients to consider 10 guidelines:

1) **Question your own history** – aim to rewrite your assumptions and consider the impact of your agendas.
2) **Practise curiosity and be courageous** – share your true thoughts in lively discussions. Also, listen carefully to others at the same time.
3) **Get comfortable with ambiguity and multiple perspectives** – organizations have as many internal futures as employees multiplied by the number of interactions they have over time, and that's before we turn to face the world.
4) **Suspend judgement** – follow the cognitive process and a rational state of mind where you actively withhold ethical judgments. Be aware of prejudgements, and bias, as these will lead you to drawing conclusions or making a judgement before having the futures narrative and all information to hand. We're not here to make decisions, just to table ideas on our futures.
5) **Be (wildly) creative** – work fast and write down as many ideas as possible, from the possible to the preposterous. Don't discount any solutions presented. Discuss them with your group and/or colleagues.
6) **Look for 'pockets of the future' in the present**[12] – look for those being wildly creative with their views on where we are going as a society. Look to poets, philosophers, writers, musicians and counter-culture creators, and listen to children's naive ideas.

[12] This one is taken from 'The eight rules of Foresight Club' by Denise Worrell, 2021, posted on LinkedIn

7) **Embrace the long-view** – if your work is starting to regress into strategic planning, i.e. things to do in the next 3 to 5 years, it's time to reset your horizons out further. When you start thinking of 50 years ahead, possible futures are still in reach, but when you push out 100, 200, 500+ years then everything is on the table for change. It's exhilarating.
8) **Focus on the non-zero-sum game** – in game theory, this is a situation in which the rewards / benefits and costs / effects experienced by all players do not balance; i.e., they add up to less than or more than zero. In these situations, the gain of one player – country, organization, community or family – is not necessarily another player's loss. It's an upside from everyone getting something or suffering dearly together. There's a romance and potent opportunity with this idea, especially when it is aligned with principles of sustainability and creating circular economy.
9) **Be careful when 'predicting' the future** – in the foresight community we insist (which academic foresight folks notably hate) that being a futurist is *not* about prediction. While I have to agree about the longer term – I would say 10+ years out – I do think that some signals are so strong that we can make broad predictions: artificial intelligence will touch every part of life, fake populism will polarize the electorate and create dangerous narratives etc. Most years I write predictions on what we'll likely see in the following year. It's easy to do that because these are more like ruminations on the signals I've been tracking, and I choose those at tipping points which take them from a quiet whisper to a loud announcement that they are here.
10) **Save *How can we make this a reality?* for last** – in your work you will be tempted to put aside the futures work and take particular ideas that may appeal and start to work out how you can make them a reality. In these cases, it's likely these are not ideas for our futures but are just extensions of existing strategic thinking or business

development activities underway. These ideas can be useful, but put them aside and tackle the wilder ideas, making *how* part of the later stages of foresight work.

Framing our thinking – from *What is* to *What if*. . .

At this point of the book, I want to share a story, a tough lesson I learnt about the development of my practice over the years.

It was early December in 2019 and I was in Calgary, Alberta preparing to speak to around 800 farmers, land investors and agricultural industrialists.

At that time, my keynotes were very much structured like lectures. *Here's the situation, what are you going to do?* It was a case of show and tell. You were either on board or not – it was provocative with little room for disputing what was being said. Sure, people could question but I would firmly state and defend my position.

At the end of that keynote, I invited questions. A middle-aged man stepped up and said, 'Everything about your talk was bullshit.' I was taken aback. There were some chuckles from the audience – some from those in sympathy with me and some in sympathy with him, made uncomfortable by what I had shared and stuck in their operational thoughts. I invited him to explain further.

He stated that the claims I was making about climate change were untrue, wasn't impressed by my views on cellular agriculture, and didn't understand why I don't consider nuclear energy to be an alternative to fossil fuels.

The next few minutes were a very public back and forth. He was clearly challenged by what I had presented, and dependent on other (perhaps conflicting) sources. I was, of course, defending what I presented.

Some 45 minutes later, I was sat in the lounge at the airport fielding a lot of troll messages on Twitter – misinformation abounds and there is a certain amount of defensiveness within the industry. Moments like this never sit well with me. It was the end of the year and I was pretty burnt out. I realized that I had to find a way to avoid these situations. I was responsible for creating this platform for discussion – and it just wasn't working.

I probably spent two or three days going through that presentation and questioning everything. I had to rethink how to present useful information and discuss our futures collaboratively. How was I to make this a platform for discussion so that even when there are disagreements, we can all get a lot from the conversation and then use those signals to question where we are today without seeking to dictate the futures ahead of us?

A few days later I was sitting in Toronto's Pearson Airport and browsing in the bookshop when one stopped me in my tracks. By the British author Rob Hopkins, it was called *From What Is to What If: Unleashing the Power of Imagination to Create the Future We Want.* Just the title alone got my mind racing and I read the opening chapters on my flight to New Orleans. Hopkins' words seemed prescient to me:

> 'In these times of deep division and deeper despair, if there is a consensus about anything in the world, it is that the future is going to be awful. There is an epidemic of loneliness, an epidemic of anxiety, a mental health crisis of vast proportions, especially among young people. There's a rise in extremist movements and governments. Catastrophic climate change. Biodiversity loss. Food insecurity. The fracturing of ecosystems and communities beyond, it seems, repair. The future – to say nothing of the present – looks grim . . .'[13]

[13] Rob Hopkins, *From What Is to What If: Unleashing the Power of Imagination to Create the Future We Want*, 2019, Chelsea Green Publishing

We do have the capability to effect dramatic change, Hopkins argues, but we're failing because we've largely allowed our most critical tool to languish - human imagination. As defined by social reformer John Dewey, imagination is the ability to look at things as if they could be otherwise. The ability to wonder *What if?*

If ever there is a time when we need that ability, it is now.

What if is an invitation to be curious without being dictatorial about what may happen in our futures. It couldn't be refuted. Any counterargument could itself be simply countered: *What if the world changed and affected your business? What if the world was different?*

That simple idea galvanized and opened my mind to the world of wider futures exploration and the role that imagination plays in futures work.

Our futures are getting brighter

If you look out into the world you'll see brands, consultancies, advertising agencies, governments and organizations starting to embrace ideas of exploring our futures. This is very encouraging, no matter what level of foresight they are applying. It shows a willingness to engage in that thought and apply futures literacy, futures design and anticipation to some of the world's greatest challenges.

Designers, developers, strategists, foresight practitioners and think tanks are coming together from diverse groups and various sectors with diverse cultural, organizational and disciplinary backgrounds and political stances. They are willing to learn and develop the ability to apply foresight methods and tools to build strategic foresight and experiential futures capabilities that serve to progress their own situations and support their needs.

The participation we see today may in part be due to the perceived glamour of futures work and the shiny futures that many are keen to share through blogs, vlogs, keynotes, social media and documentary videos. The result – unintended but useful – is that it overturns traditional thinking, and organizational leaders and governments are taking up the challenge to see beyond the next quarter or year of progress.

What I've presented in this chapter should act as a primer for you and all of these folk. So, dive in! Just remember that I have only uncovered some primary ideas and this is just 0.0001 per cent of the goodness out there.

Next we discuss our world today, how we found ourselves in this industrial complex, what keeps us caught in that web, and how we need to frame our thinking when considering positive and dystopian futures.

CHAPTER TWO

LOOKING BACK TOWARDS OUR FUTURES

In looking ahead to consider our futures we must have a reference point, an anchor for our thinking. Foresight practitioners must consider our recent histories to look ahead more effectively.

A generation which ignores history has no past – and no future.

Robert A. Heinlein

There is a simple idea that is central to my work: we must consider the context of our current situation based on historical events both macro (global and industrial) and micro (organizational, person and community). We must learn from our past mistakes so that our futures do not play out the same way.

When we start to look at horizons in our futures – 10, 20, 30+ years – I feel that we must look back 5, even 10 times further into our history to understand the trajectory and choices that were made and landed us in our current situation.

For me, the biggest question in my work is: How did we create the current reality that we are caught in today? How can we escape that industrial complex, or at least transform how it works away from its current fossil fuel-hungry, centralized form, driven by profit at all costs? Sure, profit can drive innovation, R&D and even futures work, but when organizations need to focus these are the sacrificial lambs that focus attention back to that.

Industrial Revolutions

Today, it's clear that we are caught in an industrial complex with global geopolitical tensions around energy, a supply chain that is broken and which makes little sense beyond inter-country relations, ultra-high net worth individuals (UHNWI) holding the majority of wealth in the world (also known as the '1 per cent'), misinformation peddled seamlessly via troll farms with the effect of unbalancing democracies at the voter level, the threat of more global pandemics and more. In other words, dystopia played out in reality.

On the flipside, we have seen positive progress as well over the past century – the reduction in crimes, reduced infant mortality, the speed for developing new vaccines, a decline in smoking rates, consumer prices for many goods and services have reduced, poverty is down, cancer is shifting to be a chronic condition, mRNA vaccines (for SARS-COV-19, HIV, and maybe even cancer) and more.

Industrial revolutions have transformed economies based on agrarian principles into economies based on largescale industry, mechanized manufacture and factories. Inventions and the development of new machines, fossil fuel power sources and new ways of organizing work created productive and efficient organizations and industries. As I say in my work, the dimensions of these changes accelerated and altered the exchange of information and brought new sources of energy and transportation.

The **First Industrial Revolution** started around 1765 with big changes in the three dimensions of change, most notably in terms of mechanization. At-scale agriculture started to be replaced by new industries as the backbone of our economy. Coal mining and the steam engine led to the manufacturing of railroads, thus accelerating the economy. The invention of the telegraph accelerated communications, and society shifted into factory-based economies and global trade became easier.

Almost a century later, the Second Industrial Revolution started. It was during this time that early ideas around forecasting and long-range planning emerged. In 1849, the Smithsonian Institution supplied weather instruments to telegraph companies and established an extensive observation network that submitted their observations by telegraph to the Smithsonian, where they created weather maps. I must insist that this is not *foresight*, this is *forecasting* – and the two are very different beasts. Foresight has a long view and is speculative; forecasting uses data to extrapolate what may likely come next. This is something that many people today still get very wrong and academic foresight folks become agitated at the mix-up – rightly so.

Beyond that, the period of 1870 to 1920 did lead to the birth of modern business practices and the use of forecasting more widely. Around this time, we saw the Franco-Prussian War, the formation of International Business Machines (IBM), Coca-Cola and General Electric. We also experienced more impactful stock market crashes, the Russo-Japanese War, Ford's mass production of the Model T car, and the establishment of General Motors (GM), Rolls-Royce, and Suzuki in Japan. This led to the emergence of oil-linked economies and a dependency apparent in today's economies. We also saw systematic military, urban and regional planning become widely used in the United Kingdom, Germany, France, Italy and the United States.

Notably, in the middle of this period – on 15 November 1884 – we saw the start of the Kongokonferenz, also known as the Berlin Conference. A group of ambassadors and envoys from fourteen countries – Austria-Hungary, Belgium, Denmark, France, Germany, Great Britain, Italy, Netherlands, Portugal, Russia, Spain, Sweden-Norway (unified from 1814 to 1905), Turkey and the United States – convened to discuss allowing free trade among the colonies and established a framework for negotiating future European claims in Africa. By the end of the conference European powers expanded their claims in Africa such that by 1900, European states had claimed nearly 90 per cent of African territory. For a deeper look at these events, do read 'On this day! Carving up Africa…133 years of the Berlin Conference and their license to colonize' by *New African* magazine.[14] Much of the effects of those initial conversations are still felt today across Africa, although we expect significant transformation to occur in the 2030s and beyond.

The early 1900s came on like a storm with the growth of the internal combustion engine (ICE) and more agile logistics. Modes of transportation, energy and information economies reshaped cities across the world. From 1910 to 1913 we saw the first synthetic plastic out of the USA, the nuclear model of the atom and the culmination of European militarism. Then from 1914 to 1938 we saw World War I, the Golden Twenties, the Wall Street Crash and the Great Depression.

From 1939 to 1968 we saw international conflict followed by power moves from Europe and America. Key events in this time were World War II (a time that combined the terrible loss of life with incredible innovation), followed by the Marshall Plan (known as the European Recovery Program, this was a U.S. initiative to provide aid to Europe following the devastation of the war). The Bretton Woods System created a collective international currency exchange approach that lasted from the mid-1940s to the early 1970s. There was also the establishment of the United Nations, NATO and the European Coal and Steel Community, which developed into the European Common Market. A view into our technological futures came with the development of the computer

[14] 'On this day! Carving up Africa…133 years of the Berlin Conference and their licence to colonise', 2018, *NewAfrican*

disk, the establishment of Sony, and Intel kickstarting Silicon Valley. We also saw the birth of strategic management and the first US formal military utilization of forecasting, as well as Chinese long-range science and technology efforts.

In the wake of World War II, we saw the emergence of the Third Industrial Revolution, with nuclear emerging as a transformational energy source – a subject still hotly debated today. In addition, we saw Douglas Engelbart demonstrate the world's first personal computer – mouse, desktop publishing, hyperlinking and more – in the Mother of All Demos in Stanford in 1968. It was born from thinking about human augmentation and the advancements in electronics and was the perfect companion to advancing telecommunications. Technological advancements came thick and fast via space expeditions and biotechnology. In addition, two significant inventions – Programmable Logic Controllers (PLCs) and rudimentary robotics – gave rise to an era of high-level automation. Risk and ideas of dystopia also made an entrance with early attempts at hacking and discussions around the possibility of machine superiority.

All this was a precursor to the 1990s, where we saw the public Internet and cell phones being widely used, and a world in which data fast became the new currency. Beyond Y2K we found a world open to new models of business driven by fast communications and data: the Internet Age. Douglas Rushkoff's *Cyberia* provides a fantastic view into the counterculture that was developing at that time.

Today we are firmly in the grip of the Fourth Industrial Revolution (also known as Industry 4.0). It's hard to say exactly when it started and it is a time of exponential technologies that enable complex social communications, automated transportation and the evolution of abundant renewable energy. An age where old business is at war with new business, and itself. An age where maybe true transformation is possible.

As an observer and a participant, it's easy to see how the Fourth Industrial Revolution is reshaping the world. Global economies are fast transforming to be enabled by new technologies, and projects are being implemented based on the promise of a new world. It's a technological world that is poorly considered and which has (mostly) not been designed from an ethical perspective prioritizing human needs. Unfortunately, some companies like it this way. These are the companies which, I'd argue, need foresight interventions.

We are experiencing this revolution every day, and its magnitude is yet unknown. As a foresight practitioner, this is the water I navigate trying to find a safe haven for us to dock. For the moment, though, we're at sea – and that's unlikely to change soon. Today, we need to carefully consider our futures when creating so many moving parts: the intersection of technology and humanity, transhumanism, biohacking, genetic engineering, big data, cryptocurrencies and decentralized systems, bionics, sensor fusion, machine learning and algorithms, self-aware androids, implantable technologies, wearables, virtual and augmented reality (dare I say 'the metaverse'?), the Internet of Things, and more.

It's a complex world and we are living on the edge of chaos, finding limits to our behaviours every day.

Fossil fuels and climate change – an inspiration for foresight

We need to look at the industrial revolutions and their effect on the planet and systems we rely on – pollution from industrial output and operations is a primary focus of my work. It's a perfect, albeit complex, area to look at and imagine the futures that must come after them – industry is both essential for billions of people and millions of businesses and a core pillar of global economic prosperity and function.

Without fail, each keynote and report I produce begins with global economic dynamics, climate change and the stresses on the water-energy-food nexus. The industrial complex – its benefits, opportunities, challenges and failure – can directly be tied to developments in communications, energy and transportation. These are the dimensions of change, within which there have been many inventions and innovations that come together to create momentum and change in our world.

Pollution via the burning of fossil fuels has led us to a very difficult situation, and our reliance on them is apparent. We are still in the clutch of the fossil fuel companies, depending on their supply for our transportation and heavy industry. Could undertaking foresight in this area have been useful? Yes. Was it done? Yes. What happened?

Warnings of the effects of fossil fuels emissions and climate change march firmly through our dystopian pasts. Those warnings have been ringing through time since long before political wrangling's and denial over climate change, and even before the American Civil War. In 1856 an American scientist named Eunice Newton Foote documented the underlying cause of today's climate change crisis by conducting a series of experiments that demonstrated the interactions of sunlight on different gases. Foote's scientific paper – 'Circumstances Affecting the Heat of the Sun's Rays'[15] – was the first to describe the extraordinary power of carbon dioxide gas to absorb heat. This is what we now recognize as the driving force of global warming.

Foote concluded that '… if the air had mixed with it a higher proportion of carbon dioxide than at present, an increased temperature' would result. That's some solid foresight and was

[15] Eunice Foote, 'Circumstances Affecting the Heat of the Sun's Rays', 1856, *American Journal of Science and Arts*

conveniently lost in the annuls of time, with the political modus operandi of 'wait and see'.

Throughout the late 1800s and early 1900s, science fiction and speculation emerged, but it wasn't until the late 1940s that foresight began to creep into organizational planning.[16] It began with considerations of nuclear technology, when a young analyst at the RAND Corporation, Herman Kahn, started writing short stories to outline the many possible ways that hostile nations could employ it. To help with his efforts, Kahn sought out great thinkers in the creative community near RAND's Southern California offices, such as artists, actors, screenwriters and film directors.

This work gained some attention and, in 1965, Royal Dutch Shell (RDS) developed an internal computer service, the Unified Planning Machinery (UPM),[17] which aimed to bring more discipline to their cash flow planning through the processing of large sums of data. At the same time, they started an activity out of their London headquarters called Long-Term Studies.

One of the first things RDS did was produce a Year 2000 report that aimed to develop long-term outlooks in the form of alternative futures for the company. The first oil price scenarios were sent to senior RDS executives in mid-1971. RDS' futures capability has helped shape the company's global thinking about energy, and there have been several attempts internally to shut it down. And, at no point was the suggestion made that the company needed to move wholesale away from the fossil fuels business – even though those scenarios must, I assume, have been reviewed and discussed many times, notably in terms of its negative impact on business.

---

[16] Art Kleiner, 'The man who saw the future', 2003, *Strategy+Business*

[17] Angela Wilkinson and Roland Kupers, 'Living in the Futures', 2013, *Harvard Business Review*

Short-term thinking trips up many, but it is important to note that many of these folks who have explored the future and not found answers supporting their agenda tend to root their discussions in the now. There's little more powerful than dread for our futures and the comfort of what we can do in the moment. So, good foresight work aims to challenge the now, our histories and short-term agendas – to make way for possibility. The work of lobbyists often undermines that, crafting stories to fit their agendas and imagining positive futures.

It is up to futurists to try to awaken curiosity and explore what might come to pass.

It was around the same time as RDS began its work that an American biologist Paul Ehrlich and his wife Anne wrote *The Population Bomb*, a book released in 1968. This highlighted the planet's population boom and created alarm.[18] They predicted that during the 1970s there would be societal upheaval and unrest, widespread famine, and a deterioration in environmental conditions if we did not intervene by stopping population growth and even laying down plans to reduce it.

The Ehrlichs' speculations gained a huge amount of attention – the media love a good dystopian futures story – but their fears proved wrong. They had failed to recognize that the Green Revolution had significantly increased agricultural production during in the 1960s.

In 1970, just two years after the book was published, the US biologist, geneticist and plant pathologist Norman Borlaug won the Nobel Peace Prize[19] after a career working on organizing and directing research into wheat and its production around the world. Borlaug ran the Cooperative Wheat Research and Production Program,

[18] Richard Webb, 'Paul Ehrlich: There are too many super-consumers on the planet', 2020, *New Scientist*

[19] 'Norman Borlaug: Biographical', 2022, Nobel Prize

a collaboration by the Mexican government supported by the Rockefeller Foundation. The programme involved scientific research in genetics, plant breeding, plant pathology, entomology, agronomy, soil science and cereal technology. Within 20 years Borlaug had found a high-yielding, short-strawed, disease-resistant wheat. In 25 years, cereal production increased by more than double in many parts of the world thanks to the use of modern farming technology and high-yielding varieties of wheat. Borlaug was credited with saving over an estimated billion people from starvation.

The Ehrlichs' book proved a double-edged sword, outlining scenarios that never arose thanks to Borlaug and many other scientists in the world solving difficult problems relating to caloric deficits. Their selective research created alarm and fears of rising birth rates in lower-income countries that put population control measures in place.

In 1972, a team of MIT scientists got together to study the risks of civilizational collapse and authored *The Limits to Growth*[20] – a book that was produced for the Club of Rome's project on the 'predicament of mankind'. The authors – Donella H. Meadows, Dennis L. Meadows, Jørgen Randers and William W. Behrens III – posited that the earth's interdependent resources were likely to be unable to support the then current rates of economic and population growth much beyond the year 2100. They examined the five basic factors that determine and limit growth: population increase, agricultural production, the depletion of non-renewable resources, industrial output and pollution.

The authors and their team at MIT collated and organized data related to these factors and fed them into a global computer model.

[20] Donella H. Meadows, Dennis L. Meadows, Jorgen Randers, William W. Behrens III, *Limits to Growth*, 1972, The Club of Rome

They then tested the behaviour of the model under several sets of assumptions to determine alternative patterns for humanity's future. The results showed that the outlook wasn't good. Even if we had the ability to develop advanced technology to address the problems, the researchers insisted that it would be too little, too late to make any noticeable difference.

However, in addition to the dire predictions, *The Limits to Growth* does contain a message of hope:

> 'Man can create a society in which he can live indefinitely on earth if he imposes limits on himself and his production of material goods to achieve a state of global equilibrium with population and production in carefully selected balance.'

That hope, and the analysis provided by RAND and RDS and the Ehrlichs, helped to inspire the 1970s environmental movements and the creation of organizations such as Greenpeace and Earth First!

Over the decades there have been those who choose to consider speculations on our futures as folly. I have personal experience of that. A few years back I was presenting to a group of energy executives at a retreat organized by a think tank. To prime the audience, I played a short video clip[21] from ABC News in Australia, with the journalist walking us through the data from *The Limits to Growth* and reviewing the predictions from the computer model. The presenter showed the trajectories of increasing pollution levels, population growth, reduced availability of natural resources and a diminished quality of life on earth. After 30 minutes of presenting research on climate

[21] 'Computer predicts the end of civilisation (1973) | Retro Focus', found on YouTube

change, future energy shifts to renewables, global supergrids and some scenarios on where we were heading in North America, we entered question time.

It was challenging to say the least. The fossil fuel advocates laughed and talked over the talk, while the chairman of the session disputed humanity's role in pollution and climate change. There were some in the room who were genuinely concerned about today's position, our trajectory towards levels of warming into the future, and the possibility of destabilization of global relations following the establishment of a global supergrid – an Internet of Energy.

This was par for the course in 2018. Later, in the bar, the chairman slapped me on the back and said that he was trying to be provocative. Well, that 'provocation' missed the mark. It was ignorance of the facts that were presented with no counterpoint. I suggested to him that it was dangerous to be in denial against something considered likely to challenge their industry to the core.

In 2020 Gaya Herrington provided an update to *The Limits of Growth*, publishing it in the *Yale Journal of Industrial Ecology*[22] in November of that year. It concludes that the current trajectory of global civilization is heading towards the terminal decline of economic growth within the coming decade – and at worst, could trigger societal collapse by around 2040. Her findings seem to point to how well the MIT model had stood up and how we were – through relative inaction – right on schedule.

Herrington wrote plainly in a social media post, published in 2021:[23]

[22] Gaya Herrington, 'Update to Limits to Growth: Comparing the World3 Model with Empirical Data', 2020, *Yale Journal of Industrial Ecology*
[23] Gaya Herrington, 'Beyond Growth', 2020, post on LinkedIn

> 'Amidst global slowdown and risks of depressed future growth potential from climate change, social unrest, and geopolitical instability, to name a few, responsible leaders face the possibility that growth will be limited in the future. And only a fool keeps chasing an impossibility.'

Her study represents the first time that a top analyst working within a significant mainstream global corporate entity – KPMG – has taken the *Limits to Growth* model seriously on the public stage.

In 2021 I worked with a large fruit and vegetable producer in Northern Europe. The work was to undertake research (monitoring signals and trends), train their executives in the basics of foresight, and help them run through some exercises where they envisaged their industry and business in 10+ years' time – 2031. This horizon was close enough to make them feel some conflict with their current business and far enough away so that they could start to let go of how they do things operationally and culturally today.

In the due course of research, I uncovered an incredible piece of analysis by Karl Mathiesen, Kalina Oroschakoff, Giovanna Coi and Arnau Busquets Guàrdia for POLITICO: 'Droughts, fires and floods: How climate change will impact Europe'.[24] The authors looked at data from several sources including the International Panel on Climate Change (IPCC), the European Commission, and the European Centre for Disease Prevention and Control. The article starts with strong words:

[24] Karl Mathiesen, Kalina Oroschakoff, Giovanna Coi And Arnau Busquets Guàrdia, 'Droughts, fires and floods: How climate change will impact Europe', 2021, POLITICO

> 'Climate change isn't just coming for Europe. It's coming for the European Union. Europe's north will struggle with floods and fires, even with warming at the lowest end of expectations — the Paris Agreement limits of 1.5 or 2 degrees above the pre-industrial global average. But the south will be hammered by drought, urban heat and agricultural decline, driving a wedge into one of the European Union's biggest political fault lines.'

They focused on four areas of investigation – Chapter 1: Killer Heat; Chapter 2: Hunger Games; Chapter 3: Floods and Fires; and Chapter 4: New Epidemics. The article presents some data points and potential scenarios that are worrisome, especially for those in the south of Europe:

- **Increased city heat waves** – Europe's cities could warm 6 to 10 degrees above general climate warming. The south of Europe will see the greatest increases. In Rome and other Mediterranean cities, the heat could become so intense that traditional architectural systems relying on natural ventilation will no longer function.
- **Scarce water** – At 2 degrees warming, 9 per cent of Europe's population may be competing for inadequate water supplies. In Southern Europe more than a third of the population may have less water than they need. If temperatures rise by 3 degrees, regions suffering from droughts in Europe could increase to 26 per cent, up from 13 per cent.
- **Collapsing agricultural systems and labour productivity** – Under extreme warming scenarios, southern wheat production collapses by as much as half. But even at 1.5 degrees, it will be near impossible to grow maize across much of Spain, France, Italy and

the Balkans without irrigation. In a cultural catastrophe for Italy, the best tomatoes might one day be German. Today, the heat already makes outdoor work hard and potentially deadly.

- **'Apocalypse windfalls'** – The authors state that global food supply will be squeezed, with increasing food prices delivering what they call 'an apocalypse windfall' to Northern Europe (I love a spicy metaphor in these reports). The truth is that Southern agriculture will be dying on the vine, while production moves to farmers in Ireland, Denmark and the Netherlands.
- **River flooding and rising sea levels** – If climate change continues and warming reaches 3 degrees by the end of the century, river floods could hit nearly half a million people annually – up from 170,000 now. Sea levels could rise by as much as 1.1 metres in the Mediterranean by 2100, with exposure of flooding for over 42 million people currently living in low-lying areas.
- **Lost history** – Ravenna, once the capital of the West Roman Empire, Venice, and 47 other UNESCO World Heritage sites are in the flood zones of the future.
- **New epidemics** – Heating will enable the Asian tiger mosquito to migrate and potentially spread dengue fever and West Nile virus, and a range of ticks carrying encephalitis and Lyme disease is expected to creep northward into Scandinavia.

There's no silver lining to the article – except for the farmers in Northern Europe. Rather, it highlights the need to pay attention and plan action today.

I know from experience how difficult it is to communicate reports, articles and keynotes that focus on, or even just include, some climate-related scenarios. A large percentage of the audience will likely refute them or say that the data is too speculative, or incomplete. Many times I have been bombarded with questions, statements and hokey-looking graphs without attributed research to counterpoint what I present. These days I am very careful on what sources I quote. Even to the point where I will lean into US War Army College reports for the statistics ('Implications of Climate Change for the U.S. Army'[25]). Those reports are very well researched and direct, as we might expect.

It does seem like more people now are willing to look farther ahead in relation to climate and environmental changes. There is a growing recognition that this can be an important tool in the executive's arsenal.

Thinking longer term

A by-product of these industrial revolutions is a focus on performance, profits, shareholders, quarterly targets and annual reports. These terms strike dread into my heart as a foresight practitioner.

While we may not see the end of these short-term ways of thinking in business, and the cycles they create, we certainly need to free ourselves from their constraints and think beyond them. A long way beyond them.

The industrial revolutions have both prompted and accelerated humanity's progress – and placed it under threat. One wrong move – say a global pandemic – and we quickly hit our limits and face industrial challenges – including more pollution, supply chain woes, mass resignations and more. Transformation is nowhere to be seen at that point – just reactive work schedules, plans, meetings and hope.

---

[25] 'Implications of Climate Change for the U.S. Army', United States Army War College

What Dator calls 'limits and discipline' – and a precursor to potential collapse. Not a great place to be.

Bionic companies

With the Fourth Industrial Revolution there is a need to evolve how we operate in this landscape. Many companies – from Tencent to Alphabet to Tesla to Amazon – build platforms based on data and invite users to partake in their smorgasbord of offerings, thus creating ecosystems of humanity. It's something companies fetishize – the disruptors.

To address this a new idea of modern organizational capabilities came from people at Boston Consulting Group – bionic companies. They say, 'a bionic company organizes their human and technological capabilities around business outcomes—personalizing customer experiences, improving processes, and building new offers—and moves fast to achieve them. A truly bionic company often has 30 to 50 essential processes working in this fashion.'[26]

The Japanese, and many others in Asia, are incredible long-term thinkers. Japan's SoftBank Group and their charismatic founder Masayoshi Son lean into BeCon Capital development and align that with a business plan that takes a long view; the intention is to be 'a corporate group that continues to grow for 300 years.'[27] They are aiming to create a synergetic, autonomous, decentralized and collaborative strategic group that is capable of self-evolution and self-proliferation, and which will expand to include companies that share the same aspirations. Through, I'm guessing, acquisitions and spinning off businesses developed by its $100 billion SoftBank Vision

[26] 'The Bionic Company, 2020, BCG

[27] group.softbank/philosophy/vision

Fund, which makes investments in everything from microchips, artificial intelligence and workspace to food packaging and finance.

Considering climate change – igniting conversations with a long-term view of our world

There are two speculative futures I want to highlight in the climate change area which should push our thinking towards 2200 and 2500.

The first is *Plan B: NL2200, The nation formerly known as The Netherlands*[28] which is a 'bottom-up appeal to rethink the spatial future of the Netherlands' by LOLA Landscape Architects in the Netherlands. It was based on the paper 'Impact of asymmetric uncertainties in ice sheet dynamics on regional sea level projections' by Renske C. de Winter et al.[29]

LOLA (LOst LAndscapes) presents us with a challenge:

> 'The world's best protected delta might not be able to adapt to the extreme sea-levels that could occur when the Paris climate agreements fail to sufficiently limit global temperature rise. The failure of the international climate change policy arena is unfortunately something that needs to be considered as likely to happen, while adapting dikes, dams and polders to climate change effects does have its limits.'

---

[28] 'Plan B: NL2200 – The nation formerly known as The Netherlands', LOLA

[29] Renske C. de Winter, Thomas J. Reerink, Aimée B. A. Slangen, Hylke de Vries, Tamsin Edwards, and Roderik S. W. van de Wal, 'Impact of asymmetric uncertainties in ice sheet dynamics on regional sea level projections', 2017, *European Geosciences Union*

They also provide a speculative view of our futures.

> 'Plan B envisions a Netherlands without dikes. It doesn't focus on engineering dikes and dams or constructing gigantic landfills with fossil materials from natural landscapes. Plan B uses accelerated sea level rise to leverage the rebuilding of a new Netherlands by using the driving forces of nature. In this future the Dutch would live on a logical location: above sea level, not below it.'

LOLA went to great lengths to visualize what this version of the future would look like. A shift from the coastline to the east of the country with inhabitants of the lower parts of the country moving themselves and all their facilities, infrastructures and employment opportunities.

In the east, the economic heart of the Netherlands will be reconstructed. They envisage the west coast becoming a 'marine lagoon with the protected remnants of the historic cities and villages' called 'Waterland', where residents would develop residential areas above the water, fisheries, aquaculture, energy and recreation.

In a client discussion, I brought this up briefly – it caused such an impact that we discussed the topic for over an hour, and I shared the link to the study for their consideration afterwards. Half of the executives lived in the areas affected, and I could tell behind the laughter of the scenario there was real, deep-rooted concern – not just for their business but for future generations.

Overall, this is solid futures work by LOLA, brief, well-considered and impactful. *Farewell to the Amsterdam I know and love; we had some great times together.*

With speculations like this should we try to paint a positive scenario where we've taken care of the climate crises, or outline a dystopian one? It's hard. Few sci-fi futures are overwhelmingly positive.

The second speculative future I have been using is 'Climate change research and action must look beyond 2100'[30] by Christopher Lyon et al:

> 'Anthropogenic activity is changing Earth's climate and ecosystems in ways that are potentially dangerous and disruptive to humans. Greenhouse gas concentrations in the atmosphere continue to rise, ensuring that these changes will be felt for centuries beyond 2100, the current benchmark for projection. Estimating the effects of past, current, and potential future emissions to only 2100 is therefore short-sighted. Critical problems for food production and climate-forced human migration are projected to arise well before 2100, raising questions regarding the habitability of some regions of the Earth after the turn of the century. To highlight the need for more distant horizon scanning, we model climate change to 2500 under a suite of emission scenarios and quantify associated projections of crop viability and heat stress.'

The paper uses quantitative data and projections along with some great visualizations of what we could expect if we continue our journey into the future. The authors speculate that the long-term impacts of emissions this century are likely to be felt for centuries to come, and they use three regions across the world to illustrate the effects – the American Midwest, the Amazon and the Indian subcontinent.

Today, the interior plains of the American Midwest are a global breadbasket with a climate characterized by cold winters and warm summers. In some scenarios they say we could see summer

[30] Christopher Lyon et al, 'Climate change research and action must look beyond 2100', 2021, *Global Change Biology*

temperatures increase from 28°C today to 33°C by 2100 and 36°C by 2500. This would shift what we grow and when we grow it.

The authors also look at the Amazon Basin, which is home to one-third of Earth's known species and currently serves as a carbon sink for roughly 7 per cent of anthropogenic emissions of CO_2. The region is also culturally and linguistically diverse, home to more than 350 indigenous languages. The study's modelling suggests that rising temperatures and disrupted rainfall patterns will render the Amazon Basin unsuitable for tropical rainforests by 2500, with consequences for the global carbon cycle, biodiversity and cultural diversity.

And finally, they consider Indian subcontinent. This is one of the most populous regions on Earth today and already experiences extreme climatic conditions, with thousands of deaths related to heat stress recorded between 2013 and 2015 alone. In 2022 we've seen more of the same, which has prompted a shift to night-time working to deal with the heat. Modelling suggests that mean summer monthly temperatures could increase 2°C by 2100 and 4°C by 2500, suggesting that the Indian subcontinent will experience even higher heat stress than projected for 2100.

The authors suggest several considerations for governance for long timescales:

- **Longer-term views** – A longer-term, post-2100 perspective is critical for assessing the scope of climate change on Earth systems and on human well-being.
- **Evolve International Relations** – Meeting the challenges of climate, heat stress and agricultural projections will require a major evolution in international relations away from national security and competition towards cooperation and integration (Beardsworth, 2020).

- **Shifts in the global food system** – The structure and function of the global food system will require reimagining, potentially via changes to property rights, use and ownership that mirror changes in productive climates, landscapes, populations and technologies.
- **Broader perspectives in planning** – Looking across long-term and adaptive integration of diverse cultural, knowledge and governance structures that are global in scope and approach are essential. For example, new knowledge-action synthesis efforts could inform governance institutions. These centres could be new organizations, such as long-range foresight groups or NGOs that are tied to existing governance institutions (e.g. United Nations) and networks of local governments. These cross-cultural, transnational organizations must evolve to keep ahead of observed and anticipated human migration, food production, disasters and other climate and ecological challenges. It seems like the UNFCCC is starting this effort; however, we are still on the back foot.

Even with provocative research and speculation, we see denial and inertia in acceptance that our futures may be incredibly challenging. We also see promises made and little progress pursued.

On 28 September 2021, climate activist Greta Thunberg addressed world leaders and industry alike at the Youth4Climate summit in Milan, attacking the malaise and its related spin of promises for our futures:

> 'Build back better. Blah, blah, blah. Green economy. Blah blah blah. Net zero by 2050. Blah, blah, blah. This is all we hear from our so-called leaders: words. Words that sound great but so far have not led to action. Our hopes and ambitions drown in their empty promises. Of course, we need constructive dialogue, but they have now had 30 years of blah, blah blah. And where has this led us?'

That is about as straight as we can be in terms of our current predicament. The planet is warming and it's not going to get cooler. In fact, we are on course for very difficult futures with a collapse of agricultural systems, potentially over a billion climate refugees, city infrastructure buckling (literally in some cases) under the strain of heat stress, and a litany of extreme weather events that makes the past few years of increased hurricanes, floods and wildfires look like child's play.

Repeated warnings are being shouted on the largest of public platforms. Patricia Espinosa Cantellano – the Mexican politician and diplomat who served as the executive secretary of the United Nations Framework Convention on Climate Change (UNFCCC) – reminded everyone at the opening of 2021 the United Nations Climate Change Conference, also known as COP26, on 1 November, 2021:

> 'We stand at a pivotal point in history. We either choose to achieve rapid and large-scale reductions of emissions to keep the goal of limiting global warming to 1.5°C – or we accept that humanity faces a bleak future on this planet.'

Hers was a speech delivered with the abrasiveness needed to jolt a reaction but one that was delivered on a platform where politicians prefer to dance. That's the problem. Politicians will dance and they are accompanied by teams tending to short-term thinking (encouraged by four- or five-year cycles).

What if we reframe the industrial revolutions to consider a broader worldview?

There are two things I want to reiterate at the end of this chapter: our world is changing faster than we think; it's a dangerous place determined by short-term decisions; and we must instil foresight with the intention of creating a long-term view of our futures.

Climate change and our response will continue to be a poster child for this, and I encourage focus on organizational efforts around the changes that are likely to come.

In our futures practice, I am focused on the futures of resiliency and sustainability, technologies, and cultural changes towards information, communications and useful social networks, renewable energy (wind, hydro, geothermal, centralized solar, decentralized solar and global supergrids), transportation (autonomous and last-mile logistics, airborne logistics and mobility-as-a-service), natural systems, biological advances and genetic editing. Also, our symbiotic relationship with the natural world has been pushed aside for too long.

I call this INFINITE HUMANITY – our collective potential to come together to achieve great things that support the flourishing of the human race in an equitable and empowering way.

It is a deeply humanistic, technological and spiritual practice. It is how we choose to reframe our world beyond the Fourth Industrial Revolution. I do not shy away from the challenges and risks. I embrace them as they provide cues for progressive actions we can start today. I encourage you to explore our futures, consider the trajectory you are on, and join us on this quest.

CHAPTER THREE

DON'T BE AFRAID OF THE DARK

Disrupting our base human fears prevents us from facing our challenging futures; we must face them bravely and with honesty.

'Ghost of the Future,' he exclaimed,

'I fear you more than any spectre I have seen.'

Charles Dickens, A Christmas Carol

I have accepted that dystopian futures are highly likely due to short-term thinking, ill-informed decisions and unforeseen risks. The honesty I have around this challenges people's worldview, and I'm often asked by clients for keynotes that provide an optimistic view. I have to be positive — but I also have to be realistic. I approach foresight and client work with open eyes and an open mind. I follow a rigorous process that means I struggle to get enough sleep because some things I learn along the way are very concerning.

The truth is that our futures are never convenient, and the path from today towards them will always present opportunities, challenges and risks. Futures are never what we plan for them to be, so we must entertain that there may be a balance of positive futures and dystopian possibilities – I frame this as *the darkness.*

Human limitations and human capabilities

When planning this book, I realized that there are some deeply rooted reasons why we as humans struggle to imagine our place in challenging and dystopian futures.

We've all found ourselves in situations where we freeze – either physically, or mentally. Our heads and hearts combine forces to warn: DANGER! From an evolutionary perspective this stopped us from entering situations where we could hurt ourselves or die. Over thousands of years our instincts haven't changed, but what we are fearful of has. There are no lions or venomous snakes in the grass in downtown New York City, but we fear being run over by careless drivers careering too fast through Manhattan streets.

Our modern fears are rooted in ensuring safety and having a healthy fear of the futures ahead of us that may upset our way of life – at a personal, family and community level.

The SARS-CoV-2 (Covid-19) pandemic has been the perfect storm of failed short-term thinking, policy planning, proactive futures work and base panic and knee-jerk reactions in governments and the communities they serve. Moreover, it amplified our base fears and demonstrated how often our responses are a desperate way to find control. The personal panic buying of food, sanitizers and toilet paper was an example of the futile attempt to control the path towards our futures. Neither was compromised but we couldn't stop the virus, develop vaccines or ensure the safety of the vulnerable, immunocompromised and elderly. We were forced to hide with, or without, our stockpiles. It was, quite frankly, ridiculous, and very human. It was also validating for the 'preppers' out there.

Social psychologist, broadcaster and journalist Aleks Krotoski explored our challenges in the brief and insightful article 'Your brain is temporal soup: How past narratives trap our future thoughts'.[31] Krotoski considered how challenging we found the pandemic and how our ideas of our futures are colonized by ideas from the past:

> 'If your brain is temporal soup right now, think about what we are going through. How are you going to tell the tale of COVID? Who are the major players? What advice will you pass on? When the next global health crisis comes, what will you place your faith in? Who will be valued? What role will you be allowed to play? What we imagine now changes what we can perceive, what we will imagine, and what we will be able to do.'

She talks about how our time in the pandemic has been dominated by anxiety about uncertainty. If we can tell a story that liberates the future from that one thing, then we can free ourselves, and our children, from those limiting beliefs.

That's easy to say, but not so easy in practice. Our deeply rooted fears inherited through thousands of years of survival are trapping us. Psychologists in the 20th century spent a great deal of time exploring the reasons behind our fears, the feeling of dread and the effect of learned bias on our decision making today and how we consider our futures. Carl Jung's notion of the *shadow* is central to our understanding of the human condition around fear.

However, it seems like we expend a great deal of energy trying to not consider the darkness. Messaging from politicians and positive thinkers alike reinforce the idea that if we are anticipating something positive, or a positive futures state, then we are likely to find patience or to be

[31] Aleks Krotoski, 'Your brain is temporal soup: How past narratives trap our future thoughts', 2021, *Science Focus*

inspired by our community to wait for that future. The act of waiting can itself be gratifying and reinforce positive feelings and association with those who have promised change, or things that will make our lives easier – a reduction in tax rate, industrial scale geoengineering to cool the planet, or self-driving cars that help reduce road accidents.

On the flipside, if some challenges are stated, then anxiety rises and the feelings of dread rear their ugly heads. Oftentimes these challenges cannot quickly be resolved, either – global warming, the pace and influence of misinformation, pandemics, water scarcity, cost of living etc.

Why do we find it hard as humans to embrace the possibility of bad situations? The simple answer is *bias*. With the increase in data collection, processing, accessibility and machine learning, we have seen this become a huge topic for debate over the past few years in our increasingly algorithmic world. Data and technology aside, we are influenced by three specific cognitive biases that are activated by negative news to stop us in our tracks when considering our futures.

Austin Perlmutter M.D. – author of the 'Modern Brain' series at *Psychology Today* – explores society's reaction to the modern news cycle in his article 'How Negative News Distorts Our Thinking'[32] and how that traps us in negative thinking. It's a dynamic we have witnessed in family members or colleagues, or from politicians and others. In this he highlights the three cognitive biases that are activated by negative news to keep us in a state of negativity. A state that ultimately will stop us from considering dystopian futures.

Firstly, we have **Negativity Bias**, which refers to our ability to focus on current and past negative events, information or emotions more than their positive counterparts. In modern society we feed this bias

---

[32] Austin Perlmutter, 'How Negative News Distorts Our Thinking', 2019, *Psychology Today*

and constantly reinforce that we are unable to, or will find it very difficult to, find a way out.

Secondly, we see **Availability Bias**, also referred to as the *availability heuristic*. This is the tendency for people to overestimate the importance of situations and stories that have been learned and experienced recently and so they immediately spring to mind when a decision or topic is under consideration.

Lastly, we have what we can see as the most potent: **Confirmation Bias**. Confirmation bias is the idea that people will actively seek out, remember and favour information that confirms something they already believe. In its shadow form, it is the active quest to find evidence to support negative beliefs. Something that has become easier and more complex with the saturation of good, bad, twisted and fabricated information presented via social media platforms and supported by algorithms. I have found through my work with clients that this is the biggest area which we need to address together.

Confirmation bias plays a role in business, of course. For example the business model we operate within to generate revenues, the systems we rely on – such as the internal combustion engine – and established industrial complex ecosystems we operate in – in-field vegetable growing, raising cattle for protein just like our forefathers did, logging of old growth forests to produce higher quality timber, the five-day working week, and needing to connect teams on endless Zoom calls.

No matter what is said to individuals entrenched in their confirmation biases, we are unlikely able to move them unless we get smart about it. For example, I found that talking about climate change and global warming to the agriculture and fossil fuel industries was futile unless I understood their confirmation biases and belief systems. The need to grow food using the methods passed down through generations in increasingly challenging conditions, the cost of traditional logistical methods and the heritage of the farm that their grandparents established through blood, sweat and tears. It's powerful to recognize all of these in the context of futures work and to use them as a mirror of the dynamics affecting what is happening today and the signals that indicate that change is coming.

This is something we should all do in our foresight work where the people we are working with are fixed in a loop of confirmation bias.

Challenging our beliefs

To help clients we recommend following three steps to liberate ourselves from negativity, availability and confirmation bias.

1) **Question beliefs regularly** – we must proactively question the facts on which our opinions relating to positive futures are built. We must constantly scan and listen to all sides of the arguments. It's then, when people question our beliefs, that we have a strong defence.
2) **Find evidence from like-minded people with different experiences** – in scanning for signals we can find allies in industry and academia to help communicate the importance of things likely to change. These are usually enlightened organizations and researchers that work cross-industry or are on the frontline of national security and defence (they are well funded as well).
3) **Invite people to consider alternative futures** – this is the power of shifting our mindsets from *what is* to *what if.* It's a non-committal invitation to explore new ideas at no risk to their current situations or belief systems. If we reinforce futures projects and conferences as safe spaces to explore our possible futures, we allow for a free flow of ideas and influence on how new ideas are considered in the long term. It also gives us the oxygen to consider both positive and dystopian futures without bias being as issue.

Overall, the goal of the futures work we do is to create an empathetic link between all people working on global problems and pathways to our futures with the explored realities of positive and dystopian modes and outcomes.

Empathy has long been cultivated in society, so let's look back a little further than modern psychological investigation into cultural engagement and reflection.

Framing dystopian futures

The **Johari Window,** created by psychologists Joseph Luft and Harrington Ingham in 1955, is a useful technique. It is primarily used in self-help groups and corporate settings as a heuristic exercise designed to improve self-awareness and personal development. It also helps us to better understand people's relationships and the interplay of our work within groups.

Its structure takes the form of a two-by-two grid:

	Known to self	Not known to self
Known to others	Arena	Blind Spot
Not known to others	Façade	Unknown

Fig 3.1 The Johari Window, Joseph Luft and Harrington Ingham, 1955

The two axes used in the original version by Luft and Ingham are 'Known to self' and 'Known to others'. These axes form a matrix with four quadrants and these relate to areas of exploration of our futures:

Known Knowns (the arena) are objective facts, such as easily calculable quantitative trends, shared experiences or openly accessible knowledge. Consumption trends are a good example of this. They are useful and defensible signals for consideration in futures design.

Unknown Knowns (blind spots) are too close or familiar for us to see clearly and directly. These are increasingly opaque signals that we must interpret and reflect on; apparent signals, their speculated effects and people's opinions on them. It is possible to get a deeper understanding of them through environmental scanning and various methodologies, such as weak signals analysis, horizon scanning and emerging issues analysis.

Known Unknowns (the façade) are the uncertainties we are aware of and sometimes choose to ignore. This is firmly in the realm of the futures design we undertake as we are forced to purely speculate and do not know exact outcomes. Rigorous research, knowledge management and proven methods – like the Positive-Dystopian Framework – are used to develop futures scenarios and analyze truly unexpected events.

Unknown Unknowns (unknown) are the toughest to spot. These are real blind spots and often outside the scope of our imagination. These are the events and situations that we don't even know we should be aware of or worried about. They can also be the most potent force in driving our imaginations. Unknown unknowns can be best obtained through visionary methods such as science fiction prototyping, black swan exploration (see p.81) and wild card analysis.

Often we get the Known Unknowns and Unknown Unknowns mixed up due to their uncertain nature. It was Donald Rumsfeld, the former United States Secretary of Defense, who brought these concepts to public attention in his now infamous response at a news briefing on 12 February, 2002, about the lack of evidence linking the government of Iraq with the supply of weapons of mass destruction to terrorist groups:

> 'Reports that say that something hasn't happened are always interesting to me, because as we know, there are known knowns; there are things we know we know. We also know there are known unknowns; that is to say we know there are some things we do not know. But there are also unknown unknowns – the ones we don't know we don't know. And if one looks throughout the history of our country and other free countries, it is the latter category that tends to be the difficult ones.'

We must be aware and vigilant in futures work to not let others use these as excuses and to apply them in ways that are useful versus applying them to be confusing and divisive. In the pandemic we also saw the confusion of Known Unknowns and Unknown Unknowns with SARS-CoV-2 being called a *black swan* – a metaphor popularized by Nassim Nicholas Taleb in his 2007 book of the similar name, referring to unanticipated events with big impacts. Pandemics have been inconvenient but expected over time, so they are Known Unknowns and not black swan events. We often refer to these as described as the *black elephants* in the room – dangerous and apparently unpredictable but in fact predictable if we choose to pay attention.

The Johari window and definitions have been useful in futures design, and foresight researchers and practitioners have tried their best to create metaphors to describe them to aid in recall and consideration.

The paper 'The Three Tomorrows of Postnormal Times'[33] by Ziauddin Sardar and John A. Sweeney identifies a 'menagerie of postnormal potentialities' which they 'developed as a mechanism for challenging deeply held convictions, illuminating entrenched contradictions, and enlivening novel considerations.'

Sardar developed the *Postnormal Times* concept so that we can operate and analyze situations 'in an in-between period where old orthodoxies are dying, new ones have yet to be born, and very few things seem to make sense.' This is a useful way to navigate and consider futures scenarios with Unknown situations by understanding the transition between states of now and our futures.

Sardar and Sweeney identify three metaphorical animals to help with framing and considering postnormal futures. These relate nicely to three of the segments presented by the Johari Window.

Black Elephants are a sort of Known Unknown. These events with high postnormal potential require collective, global action – like pandemics. Black elephants capture the postnormal dynamic of the *Extended Present*. They are decidedly contextual – in the now and our near futures – and must be approached from more than one perspective in order to capture the contradictions and conditions inherent to their emergence.

[33] Ziauddin Sardar and John A. Sweeney, 'The Three Tomorrows of Postnormal Times', 2015, *Futures*

Black Swans are fundamentally Unknown Unknowns. In contrast to black elephants, Black Swans might be negative or positive. Their impact might highlight previously unimagined opportunities, which is what suits them for the complex dynamics of exploring our future(s). Indeed, it has been argued that black swans are responsible for some of the greatest societal changes of history.

Black Jellyfish are the Unknown Knowns. Things we think we know and understand but which turn out to be more complex and uncertain than we expect. 'Black Jellyfish are all about how normal situations and events become postnormal.' Sardar and Sweeny say that 'demonstrating how small things can have a big impact driven by positive feedback, jellyfish blooms provide us with the ideal representation of postnormalcy in the unthought future(s).'

These metaphors save a great deal of time in explaining the concepts to clients wanting to understand the nuance of the knowns and unknowns. With better understanding of these, and an embracing of the state of *Postnormal Times*, we can better prime thinking and pushing of boundaries when we approach scenario design, and spark useful discussions around the shape and trajectory of our futures.

Resilience, the mantra for the next 100 years

We must recognize the importance of considering both dystopian and positive futures critically and with open hearts and minds. Understanding the bias and frameworks somewhat help us develop ability to empathize with both versions of our futures.

I've always stated to clients that courage is an important part of working in futures design. I confront what people believe their future to be and invite them to consider our futures and what may happen. I have found the biggest challengers to ideas of our futures when presenting to larger audiences. Deindividuation and the support by proxy of being in a room with others provides individuals with the courage to say, 'I don't believe you,' or 'I'm fearful of the future you're speaking about.' I remind people that nothing is set and these are speculations, and if the signals and speculations I share are unsettling to your organization, then we must together go deeper in that exploration of why.

In addition, I keep asking what if our world, and our life, was made different by societal changes, systematic shifts, and a change in how the world operates.

It's impossible to travel backwards in time, and we live with the decisions we all make – from systems that are implemented to policy and regulation. What this provides is the opportunity to reflect and consider how those foundations will help us consider the futures that we can imagine ahead of us.

Our futures are rarely convenient, so we need to explore what might be, get ready for change, and become resilient through transformation. That resiliency means that we must constantly transcend our fears, frame positive futures, consider the pathways to dystopian futures, and add rigour, clinical thinking and creativity to our approaches.

CHAPTER FOUR

LESSONS FROM THE FRONTLINES

The world of the dystopian challenges we face today could have been anticipated using foresight. In many cases it was, and the warning signs were ignored in favour of 'progress'.

In order to rise from its own ashes, a Phoenix first must burn.

Octavia Butler

There are many lessons from history of mistakes made and of short-term thinking leading to unchecked progress and cultural influence. There is always the opportunity to use foresight to explore what challenging situations may arise, to anticipate unforeseen risks and to understand future scenarios, and complex stories, where both opportunities and great challenges exist.

We've already discussed population growth, agriculture and food supply, the water-energy-food nexus, and longer-term thinking around climate futures. However, there are some other parts of society that should be brought into focus in terms of their history, developments, use of foresight, and the ignorance of what might come from the short-termed, ill-informed or blind decisions being made today.

We will explore three somewhat interlinked areas that impact nearly everyone on the planet: pandemic preparedness; the Internet and the influence of Big Tech; and multi-generational trauma and our mental health.

Pandemic preparedness

SARS-CoV-2 (Covid 19), a global pandemic that sprung up in late 2019, has us questioning how so much of our society works. Should we have expected the events that have transpired? Could we have speculated on the challenges and opportunities that have presented themselves?

Absolutely. A number of clear signals indicated that this was very likely.

The world has a long history of pandemics over the years, and especially so in the last hundred or so years – Spanish Flu, Hong Kong Flu, HIV/AIDS, SARS, MERS, Zika, Ebola, and now Covid-19 (and its variants). Many warned that a respiratory virus would cause havoc in society, leading to hundreds of millions of infections and millions of deaths.

Urban centres are growing and encroaching on our wildlife habitats – where it's estimated that seven million or more zoonotic viruses exist. The travel between rural and urban centres and exotic meat food supply (bushmeat etc.) has been increasing (certainly in Asia and Africa). Global travel and trade have created an ecosystem for transmission we've never seen before. So, in late 2019 when we saw initial signs of a new epidemic in Wuhan, China and the silencing of journalists, bloggers and doctors, we should have been ready. The world watched and waited with many powerful world leaders in a state of refusal, denying its potential effects and hoping that it would magically disappear.

What's interesting is that pandemics have been one of the areas that foresight has looked at over the past few years. Ed Yong, a journalist for *The Atlantic* who has written much about the SARS-CoV-19 pandemic, wrote a prescient piece in 2017 called 'Is It Possible to Predict the Next Pandemic?'[34] The article taps into the wisdom of many researchers that have been working in this space and looks at initiatives like PREDICT[35] – an initiative with extensive funding from the U.S. Agency for International Development which has identified nearly 1,000 new viruses – and The Global Virome Project[36] – 'a collaborative scientific initiative to discover zoonotic viral threats & stop future pandemics'. Yong spoke with Kevin Olival from EcoHealth Alliance, who works with PREDICT and says that it would be impractical to study all scenarios and potential 'fault-lines'. 'We need tools to help us narrow down and target our resources to the locations, host species, and viruses of greatest concern.' Projects like PREDICT and the Global Virome Project may not act as crystal balls for future outbreaks, but they 'help us prioritize on-the-ground disease surveillance.' This sounds like a job for scenario exploration and futures design to complement the scientific disciplines already at play.

The UK government did just this in 2016. Dame Sally Davies was the chief medical officer who commissioned a health planning exercise – called Exercise Alice[37] – that imagined a coronavirus outbreak. Davies and her team worked with officials from NHS England, the Department of Health, Public Health England and observers from the other administrations.

The final report states that 'the scenario for Exercise Alice was designed to explore existing arrangements and to scrutinize the

[34] Ed Yong, 'Is It Possible to Predict the Next Pandemic?', 2017, *The Atlantic*

[35] USAID PREDICT, 'Program Info', EcoHealth Alliance

[36] www.globalviromeproject.org

[37] Public Health England's Emergency Response Department, 'Report – Exercise Alice Middle East Respiratory Syndrome', 2016, Public Health England

challenges presented by a large-scale MERS-CoV outbreak in the UK. Specifically, it aimed to explore what the options were and to assess what was already in place to manage such an incident.' Some clear directives came from the report:

- We will require access to sufficient levels of appropriate PPE, and pandemic stockpiles were suggested as a means to ensure sufficient quantities were available.
- There is a requirement for early command and control and the need to coordinate the response.
- We need to develop the capability for contact tracing and quarantining
- There will be a desirability of exploring new or experimental therapies and treatments and considering initiating early or fast track clinical trials as a priority.

The *Guardian* featured a story about this in their article 'Coronavirus report warned of impact on UK four years before pandemic' and the fact that exercises like this were not acted upon.[38] When they questioned a spokesperson for the Department of Health and Social Care, they said that Exercise Alice 'was not a coronavirus pandemic preparedness exercise' as it was based on a scenario using Middle East Respiratory Syndrome (MERS) as the viral respiratory illness of concern.

While there are some clear differences between MERS and SARS-CoV-2 – i.e., it does not transmit as easily and the risk profile is different – this could've led to the development of a coordinated and

[38] Robert Booth, 'Coronavirus report warned of impact on UK four years before pandemic', 2021, *Guardian*

proactive capability which might have reduced the mortality rate of SARS-CoV-2 in the UK, and maybe in other countries too.

I was approached by a large technology company in September 2019 to plan for global expansion and consider the signals and trends that indicate change over the next 30 to 50 years. I produced a global research report that delved into population growth, global and national security and the water-energy-food nexus, and which looked for opportunities for expansion in strategic regions. It considered the cultures, countercultures and black-market underbellies of these places. I presented the findings in December 2019, and in February 2020 we checked in on the work to discuss next steps during a trip I had planned in New York City.

'Where was the mention of pandemics in your report?' they said, laughing. We all did. SARS-CoV-2 was yet to come to North America in any way that caused concern. I had created an addendum and presented it at that meeting. I'll be honest, it was brief and understated. I also met with several *Wall Street Journal* reporters to discuss futures planning and issues. Again, no real attention was paid to the potentiality of a pandemic causing significant disruption.

About six weeks later North America was descending into lockdown, and I was sitting in my home office contemplating what to do next as all my client work evaporated. Conferences and events were cancelled indefinitely and many clients cancelled external initiatives.

I called my client in New York City, and they commissioned me to work with them on emerging challenges and scenarios relating to the pandemic. We all had to ignore the political noise and look the pandemic in the face and work out what dimensions of change would be important, and what would likely transpire over time. I focused on working collaboratively with my client and digging into significant signals that were emerging in a number of areas:

- **Medicine and healthcare** – the risk of new zoonotic diseases entering society beyond SAR-CoV-2, new at-work health protocols and biomedical preparedness, wearables, addiction and mental health.
- **Water-energy-food nexus** – drought, famine and locust plagues, climate change, food systems, a struggling supply chain and the fiscal effects of inflation.
- **Business operations and technology infrastructure** – virtual engagement and tactical user experience, the future of collaborative and nomadic work, urbanization, city and office design, construction, technology infrastructure impacts.
- **Citizen movements, crime and policing** – civil unrest, the rise of decentralized militias and their coordination to attack governmental institutions (we had seen significant evidence that something like the attacks on 6 January 2021 were likely to happen), organized crime and cybercrime, gun sales indicating a rise in gun-related crimes, the need for 'mass-shooting insurance', the drive and impact of Black Lives Matter accelerating, 'defunding the police', and so much more.

My client and I gained foresight that the complexity of the COVID-19 pandemic is impressive and terrible. The reports we produced were prescient. Many of the things we said would accelerate and impact the world have come to pass. It also motivated my client to seek more training and become the futurist-in-residence within that client's business unit, where they continue the work.

Out of all the research there was one organization that was prepared for a pandemic of this magnitude. From 2002 to 2004 the SARS epidemic had created some challenges for the All-England Lawn Tennis Club and their Grand Slam tennis tournament Wimbledon. They decided to take precautionary action and pay for pandemic insurance to safeguard against future disruptions. For 17 years they paid for an insurance policy to guard against losses if the tournament should have to be cancelled in the event of a worldwide pandemic. In 2020 they reportedly received a payment worth $141 million – about half the amount that the club expected to lose because of the cancellation.

For me, that was foresight in action. The preparedness of countries like Singapore, Taiwan and South Korea are notable as is the direct action of places like New Zealand where they have a solid future thinking capability in government[39] to inform policy decisions. Civic responsibility, solid government policy and decisive leadership were critical, and lacking in so many parts of the world due to the malaise of short-termism.

The pandemic has made every government and organization step up and ask if their strategic planning goes far enough and whether they need to invest in more capabilities around scenario planning and futures design. The pandemic has been like steroids for my business. In 2020 and 2021 I expanded my team and we worked with central banks, credit card companies, global insurance associations, industrial-scale food producers, franchise associations and large multinational retailers, cities across North America, and multi-billion-dollar aerospace companies. The work was serious foresight and futures design. With each engagement we teach them the basics of scanning for signals, identifying trends and writing scenarios.

More than anything, this work inspired me to write this book; there are many more organizations and governments out there needing to create a longer view on positive and dystopian futures.

---

[39] 'Futures Thinking', Department of the Prime Minister and Cabinet – New Zealand Government

Rise of the Internet and the influence of Big Tech

In 1957, an engineer and inventor called Douglas Engelbart, mentioned earlier, started working on human-computer interaction at Stanford Research Institute (SRI) in Menlo Park, California. He worked on several notable and experimental projects and in 1962 produced a report about his vision and proposed research agenda: 'Augmenting Human Intellect: A Conceptual Framework.'[40] It was a paper that explored the need for augmenting our intellect and laid down an important and impactful final thought:

> 'After all, we spend great sums for disciplines aimed at understanding and harnessing nuclear power. Why not consider developing a discipline aimed at understanding and harnessing "neural power"? In the long run, the power of the human intellect is really much the more important of the two.'

Engelbart had laid out a challenge to use technology to level up humanity. Then after several years of research into how we could augment our intelligence, and the invention of a then-strange control device called the 'mouse', he gave a demonstration at the Association for Computing Machinery / Institute of Electrical and Electronics Engineers Computer Society's Fall Joint Computer Conference in San Francisco on 8 December 1968. This demonstration became known as the Mother of All Demos. Engelbart's live demonstration featured the introduction of a complete computer hardware and software

[40] Douglas Engelbart, 'Augmenting Human Intellect: A Conceptual Framework', 1962, Doug Engelbart Institute

system called the oN-Line System or, NLS as it came to be known. Engelbart began the presentation:

> 'I think the research program that I'm going to describe to you is quickly characterized by saying, if in your office, you as an intellectual worker, were supplied with a computer display, backed up by a computer that was alive for you all day, and was instantly responsible, responsive, instantly responsive, every action you had, how much value could you derive from that?'

The 90-minute presentation unveiled fundamental elements of modern personal computing: a windows-based interface with efficient navigation and command input (from keyboard, control pad and computer mouse), graphics, video conferencing, word processing, hypertext, dynamic file linking, revision control and a collaborative real-time editor that hinted at how we could work collaboratively. The underlying technologies influenced both the Apple Macintosh and Microsoft Windows graphical user interface operating systems that were developed in the 1980s and 1990s.

Search for the video of the Mother of All Demos and imagine what it would have been like seeing it for the first time and wondering what if this changes business and humanity? What if there was mass-adoption of these technologies? What if entire global economies change?

Like any new vision of what our futures may be, it had its detractors. The pioneers of business computing insisted that personal microcomputing was an unlikely future to expect. Ken Olsen, the then President of DEC (Digital Equipment Corp.), gave a presentation to the World Future Society in 1977 and declared, 'there is no reason for any individual to have a computer in his home'. Apparently, he began to change his mind when he saw several personal computers used to control homes and other useful applications, and after his daughter begged him to buy her a computer to use at home.

Around the same time, the ARPANET was in development. I'll not be outlining its history, so if you're looking for a primer on the Internet before it went public, refer to The Internet Society's article 'Brief History of the Internet'.[41] On 30 April 1993 the European Organization for Nuclear Research (CERN) put the web into the public domain, with key protocols developed by Sir Tim Berners-Lee.

In 1995 an essay by media theorists Richard Barbrook and Andy Cameron of the University of Westminster was released on Metamute called 'The Californian Ideology'.[42] They argued that 'the rise of networking technologies in Silicon Valley in the 1990s was linked to American neoliberalism and a paradoxical hybridization of beliefs from the political left and right in the form of hopeful technological determinism.'

> 'The California Ideology is a mix of cybernetics, free market economics, and counter-culture libertarianism and is promulgated by magazines such as *WIRED* and *MONDO 2000* and preached in the books of Stewart Brand, Kevin Kelly and others. The new faith has been embraced by computer nerds, slacker students, 30-something capitalists, hip academics, futurist bureaucrats and even the President of the USA himself. As usual, Europeans have not been slow to copy the latest fashion from America. While a recent EU report recommended

[41] Barry M. Leiner, Vinton G. Cerf, David D. Clark, Robert E. Kahn, Leonard Kleinrock, Daniel C. Lynch, Jon Postel, Larry G. Roberts, Stephen Wolff, 'Brief History of the Internet', 1997, Internet Society

[42] Richard Barbrook and Andy Cameron, 'The Californian Ideology', 1995, Mute

adopting the Californian free enterprise model to build the "infobahn", cutting-edge artists and academics have been championing the "post-human" philosophy developed by the West Coast's Extropian cult. With no obvious opponents, the global dominance of the Californian ideology appears to be complete.'

Technolibertarianism was fuelled by data and networked connections. Everyone – of all beliefs and political positions – was invited to the party. Sure, there were principles: the policy should always be considerate of civil liberties; the policy should oppose government over-regulation; and a policy that provides rational, free market incentives is the best choice.

If you've ever spent time in Silicon Valley or San Francisco, then you'll be familiar with the people who typify this, and the feeling and drive that still exist in the beating hearts of the Patagonia-clad venture capitalists, start-ups and tech behemoths – and their easy smiles that promise: 'Everything is going to be OK'.

To see the fervour, excitement and juggernaut energy of those early days, do seek out Ondi Timoner's documentary *We Live in Public*, where she follows 'the greatest Internet pioneer you've never heard of,' Josh Harris.

After founding the technology market research consulting firm Jupiter Communications, Harris founded Pseudo.com, an early version of Internet lifestyle programming. He then went on to become interested in controversial human experiments which tested the effects of media and technology on the development of personal identity in his art project 'Quiet: We Live in Public'. This was a surveillance-driven concept that invited over one hundred artists to live in a bunker under New York City surrounded by hundreds of cameras. Harris deliberately set the tone of the Internet to come, and I do not think it was a throwaway phrase – it was an instruction manual:

> 'Everything is free except the video we capture of you. That we own.'

If that wasn't a signal of what was to come, then I don't know what was.

During this time, what we call Web 1.0 was well underway. An Internet with millions of static pages and content served from central servers' file systems, where webpages were built using Server Side Includes (SSI), and where frames and tables were used to position and align the elements on a webpage. This was a foundational web, where personal web pages were common with static pages hosted by Internet Service Providers (ISPs) or on free web hosting services.

I built several static sites within Geocities, an early web hosting service that allowed users to create and publish websites for free and to browse user-created websites by their theme or interest. I used these sites to share ideas and host my own electronic music. The community was growing, and organizations were starting to host websites. Go and check out the Internet Archive – The Wayback Machine[43] – to look at the websites built back then by Microsoft, AOL and other companies. 'Surfing the Internet' was a thing and having access to information quickly and accessing new dot-com businesses was the flavour of the day.

In 1996 the Communications Decency Act came into effect in the United States, which many saw as a threat to the independence

[43] The Wayback Machine – https://archive.org/web/

and sovereignty of cyberspace. In response John Perry Barlow of the Electronic Frontier Foundation (EFF) presented A Declaration of the Independence of Cyberspace:[44]

> 'Governments of the Industrial World, you weary giants of flesh and steel, I come from Cyberspace, the new home of Mind. On behalf of the future, I ask you of the past to leave us alone. You are not welcome among us. You have no sovereignty where we gather.
>
> 'We have no elected government, nor are we likely to have one, so I address you with no greater authority than that with which liberty itself always speaks. I declare the global social space we are building to be naturally independent of the tyrannies you seek to impose on us. You have no moral right to rule us nor do you possess any methods of enforcement we have true reason to fear.'

Certainly a defence of the fundamentals behind the Californian Ideology, this was one of the pushbacks from those that wanted the Internet to be a wholly free space. A noble idea not readily accepted by the government who wanted to control it rather than imagine what it truly could be.

The Dot-com Bubble eventually burst, with many of the well-funded start-ups running out of runway due to a lack of consumer needs and failed business models — curious how many overenthusiastic founders had shiny, brand-new Porsches. Some companies that we still see today did endure, although it was not an easy time.

Next came Web 2.0. This became known as the 'social web' – which offered worldwide websites that had user-generated content

---

[44] John Perry Barlow, 'A Declaration of the Independence of Cyberspace', 1996, *EFF*

(UGC), usability and interoperability for the browsers of the sites. This marked the beginning of social networks where personal social graphs were cultivated and connections were made using platforms for podcasting, blogging; tagging; RSS, social bookmarking, social networks and social media, and web content voting. Tim O' Reilly, who popularized the term *Web 2.0*, said:

> 'Web 2.0 is the business revolution in the computer industry caused by the move to the Internet as a platform, and any attempt to understand the rules for success on that new platform.'

Web 2.0 has evolved greatly over the years and many of the platforms seen in the early days have persevered, or inspired a multitude of new platforms: hosted services (Google Maps); web applications (Google Docs, Software as a Service platforms); video sharing sites (Vimeo and YouTube), wikis (Wikipedia and Wikimedia), blogs (WordPress), messaging (WhatsApp and Signal), microblogging (Twitter), podcasting (Podcast Alley), content hosting services, and the modern might of social networking (Facebook, Instagram, Snap, TikTok).

Much like the early 1990s and the mid-2000s, we find ourselves today in an excited feeding frenzy of tech companies, new and ever-evolving social networks, content platforms, and the 'as-a-service' companies offering the connection of financial, transportation, community, business administration, and other useful applications. It's an interesting time and many of my clients and media outlets ask me to dissect what is going on and to identify what is noise and hype versus what will likely continue and create lasting cultural changes.

The signals from Engelbart's original demo – personal computing as a functional rich and useful tool for everyone; Web 1.0 – access, freedom of information sharing, and government intervention; and Web 2.0 – social connection and influence – were apparent, but few organizations and governments were wondering what might happen in the next 10, 20 and 30+ years. The philosophies of 'move fast and break things' from the poster children of this new age – Facebook, Google, Amazon et al., – drove progress more than careful consideration of what might result from these networks and repositories of images, data and metadata.

We should have anticipated and considered scenarios that contained what has come to pass. A technocratic free-for-all where growth at any cost rules the strategy decks presented to venture capitalists to liberate billions of dollars from the investor funds looking for 10x and even 100x returns. We should have considered what would be wrought upon society with these cultural disruptors: the formalization and growth of the cloud infrastructure shared by many critical services we use; the amplification of societal issues around interpersonal and customer to business relationships; the accidental creation of zero day bugs and vulnerabilities; the rise of foreign-state actors, and independent hacker collectives looking to hold society's infrastructure (schools, hospitals, the water-energy-food nexus) hostage; the dopamine addictions created by viral double-loops capturing and keeping our children's attention; mobile devices that are seldom left alone; and, so much more.

Today's Internet is wild and vibrant. Each day we see over 5.2 billion Internet users, nearly 2 billion websites, 170 billion emails per day, 4.9 million blog posts written, 60m Instagram uploads, 4.9 billion YouTube video views, 133k websites hacked, 2.6 million cell phones sold, and, perhaps most worryingly, 2.2 million tons of CO_2

emissions – all statistics courtesy of Internet Live Stats.[45] Ultimately it is a battleground for hearts, minds and wallets. It's also a place that very literally makes and breaks modern organizations, and it has a cascading effect on most of society.

From this we have found ourselves part of a complex web of algorithms and in Web 3.0 – a hyper-connected, visually rich place driven by sensor fusion and with the potential for mass decentralization. These are semantic webs supported by machine learning (Artificial Intelligence), 3D graphics, connectivity through a multitude of devices (mobile, virtual and augmented reality headsets, wearables and implanted technologies), ubiquitous two-way access, accessible content, and cryptocurrencies / blockchain technologies (and their derivative platforms).

It's an ecosystem built on the strongest currency in the world: data. The growth of that is exponential – a word that makes venture capitalists and start-ups excited – and we expect that there will be over 175 zettabytes of data created each year, a CAGR of 61 per cent up from up from 33zb of data in 2018 (source: IDC)[46] and an expected 4,900 digital data engagements per person each day by 2025 – that's approximately one digital interaction every 18 seconds.

Web 3.0 is a world accelerated by thousands of algorithms that guide our lives, and it's still a struggle for independence – now a theme that's carried through since the early days of the Internet and designed by those with little consideration of our futures. There are many critics of the algorithms that are ripping through society unchecked, as stated by Cathy O'Neil the author of *Weapons of Math Destruction: How Big Data Increases Inequality and Threatens Democracy*:

---

[45] Stats taken from www.internetlivestats.com

[46] 2021, 'Rethink Data', Seagate

> 'The math-powered applications powering the data economy were based on choices made by fallible human beings. Some of these choices were no doubt made with the best intentions. Nevertheless, many of these models encoded human prejudice, misunderstanding, and bias into the software systems that increasingly managed our lives. Like gods, these mathematical models were opaque, their workings invisible to all but the highest priests in their domain: mathematicians and computer scientists. Their verdicts, even when wrong or harmful, were beyond dispute or appeal. And they tended to punish the poor and the oppressed in our society, while making the rich richer.'

Web 3.0 has become chaos fuelled by big technology, disruptive start-ups and organizations with secretive founders. It's also fuelled by big money, influencers and organizations trying to win the hearts and minds of the young. It's about the rise of virtual economies which are having impacts on real-world economies, e.g. Roblox and its inclusion of high-price luxury goods from brands like Gucci, or Fortnite selling skins to players.

Edward Castronova is a professor of media at Indiana University Bloomington and is known for his work on the economies of synthetic worlds. Back in 2002 – a time when Web 2.0 was starting to accelerate and online gaming economies started to gain pace – he wrote a paper, 'On Virtual Economies',[47] sharing his thoughts on what might happen if virtual worlds become populous and places for occupation, work and business:

[47] Edward Castronova, 'On Virtual Economies', 2002, Center for Economic Studies and ifo Institute (CESifo)

> 'If virtual worlds do become a large part of the daily life of humans, their development may have an impact on the macroeconomies of Earth. It will also raise certain constitutional issues. . .'

In our modern tech-driven world, the enabler of a global virtual economy can be seen as what people are hailing as the *metaverse*. A world that transcends online and offline worlds, where true creativity and freedom of thought has been squeezed out by the conformity of alternative arts, music, places and, ultimately, people. We are at that point today, exemplified by the full-tilt movement of many significant big tech players into virtual worlds – Meta, Microsoft, Alphabet, Sony, Roblox, and Epic Games to name a few – and of the founders and disciples of cryptocurrency.

These are some of the corporations trying to create streams of revenues and exponential growth by embracing decentralization and applying centralized economic rules to collect earnings, convert to fiat currencies and recognize them on the balance sheet. A digital chimera of sorts.

Watching the daily chatter around Web 3.0 – from decentralization to the metaverse – is intoxicating for some because the technologies within are held up as the liberators of society. For others – myself included – it's a terrifying descent into unbridled anarchy that will become stifled by old-style regulation written by those who can barely write and send an email let alone manage a crypto wallet or mint an NFT. Web 3.0 is the *speculative web* promoting personal empowerment while maintaining control through anonymity and crypto whales (individuals or entities holding large amounts of cryptocurrency). It uses umbrella terms like *metaverse* to obfuscate and distract us from critical thinking on how it works and what it means for our futures.

I spend a lot of my time wondering where this ends, if at all. I feel that the Internet today and the Web 3.0 hype is careering us towards its logical conclusion – humanity as an active layer in the product. Keeping in with the theme of positive and dystopian futures, I wanted to find a term that lends itself to an overall feeling. For this digital foundation, feeling and place, I've chosen the term *Notopia*, used in 2007 by Fivos Papadimitriou in his article 'A geography of "Notopia" – Hackers et al., hacktivism, urban cyber-groups/cyber-cultures and digital social movements':[48]

> 'The expansion of information and telecommunication technologies has resulted in the emergence of new urban virtual cultures, while the social, technological and economic impacts of these cyber-cultures have already been felt. This study categorizes and gives the main characteristics of some urban cyber-groups and cyber-cultures (for instance, categories of hackers, hacktivists) and attempts to explore their activities as emerging urban social movements. These activities take place in a sub-space of the Internet, which we may name "Notopia" (no + topos, in Greek μη τόποϛ), this being a space of unmapped, unidentifiable, nameless places. It is suggested that cyber-groups/cyber-cultures might be explained by the ideologies they often subscribe to, whilst the structural aspects of urban cyber-cultures should be examined in more detail, so as to derive a better understanding of their social characteristics and thus, of our future digital cities.'

The description of 'a space of unmapped, unidentifiable, nameless places' resonated with me as I considered Web 3.0, so I have co-opted

[48] Fivos Papadimitriou, 'A geography of "Notopia", 2007, *City*

the term, with respect. I state that Notopia is a consequence of the cold logic of market forces combined with a populace that is disinterested and apathetic on the one hand, and highly motivated and activistic on the other. I provide a definition, to be referenced, as follows:

> 'Notopia is a nowhere place devoid of pathos where nothing truly exists, and nobody really matters. A place that is populated by "users" that are layers in technical architecture, where the algorithms rule, and the teams of people behind it actively manipulate behaviour, data, and psychologies. A place where liberty and democracy exist only within the forms of the platforms and groupthink controlled by the platforms themselves. A place where people perceive value creation online that bleeds into the real world to only have it snatched from them due to the changing operations and whims of the technocratic masters.'

Notopia is dystopian by nature and decorated as a 'perfect new place', when in fact it is no place at all and we are the 'children of the algorithm', struggling to break free. This reflects and advances the old struggles of the Internet – of freedom and the perceived need for control – into the real-world dynamics of hierarchy of wealth and status. It's also a place where users are subject to corporate surveillance, a 'firehose' of information, disempowering data collection and usage policies, new tools for social engineering and troll farms, a multitude of parasocial relationships, upturned ethics, and – at worst – digital addiction and digital dementia.

Notopia is as much about the problem, the opportunity and the call for action. I could continue to discuss this further but I'll move on and leave that to be an area of exploration in the future.

Multigenerational trauma and mental health

Trauma is deeply rooted and pervasive, and it affects all of us, even on the happiest and best days of our lives. From those who were caught in abusive situations, whose parents suffered the trials of war, those who left their mental health unchecked for most of their lives.

My work is deeply informed by trauma. Most people's work is as well. Our experiences, and those of parents, grandparents, and generations prior to them have shaped who we are fundamentally.

Imagine nearly eight billion people and what multigenerational trauma they carry. We're caught in our own bodies and there's a metaphysical way out if we choose to pursue it. In most cases, it's brushed off as being 'who we are'. I place multigenerational trauma and the resulting mental health challenges at number one in terms of the most important challenges to address. It's shaped the short-term political thinking, the ego decisions, the greed, the wars, the conflict in life.

It's impacting us right now and we will likely feel it through the day manifesting as stress, insomnia, bad habits and cries for help. We can see people struggling every day and we need to dial up empathy and connections with even the most challenging of individuals.

In late 2019 I released a study into the future of life in America[49] with my friend Nick Black. When we analyzed the results from surveying 2,025 United States residents, we found that things were not so great from a mental health perspective. Younger Americans were reporting significantly higher rates of life stress. Among those aged 16 to 29, almost half (48 per cent) reported experiencing financial stress most or every day, 43 per cent reported experiencing family stress most or

---

[49] Nick Black and Nikolas Badminton, 'Future of Life in America: 2020 Report', 2020, *Intensions*

every day, and 35 per cent reported experiencing work stress most or every day.

Younger Americans were also more likely to report significantly higher rates of loneliness and insecurity, with 47 per cent often feeling isolated from other people, 47 per cent often feeling left out by other people, 50 per cent often worried that other people were judging them, and 40 per cent often worried that other people might hurt them. Black elaborated:

> 'These findings show a real disparity between the sense of safety and connection reported by older Americans, and the sense of insecurity and loneliness reported by younger Americans. It appears that many young Americans are experiencing a deep sense of disconnection.'

The study also found that younger Americans were more likely to have experienced mental health problems. Among those aged 16 to 29, 31 per cent had been diagnosed or treated for anxiety in the past year, 29 per cent had been diagnosed or treated for depression in the past year, and 30 per cent self-identified as narcissists (e.g. egotistical, self-focused, vain).

I saw that young adults born in the Internet Age had been promised an exciting and connected future. Instead, we've seen reduced privacy, greater exposure to disinformation and more fragile mental health. There needs to be a shift towards reconnecting with the friends, families and communities that support mental resiliency.

This study was also pre-pandemic, so I find myself imagining how all these indicators have dialled up today and wondering about the effects on their personal life and the organizations within which they work.

In the UK the *Guardian*[50] reported on NHS data that showed there has been a 29 per cent increase in the number of people with their first suspected episode of psychosis between April 2019 and April 2021. And in the article 'Mental Health in America: A Growing Crisis',[51] *Psychiatric Times* reports that increased mental health care needs at a time of increasingly restricted access are likely to lead to unknown long-term consequences. More specifically, the US Center for Disease Control (CDC) saw that from August 2020 to February 2021 there was 'an increase in the proportion of adults reporting recent symptoms of anxiety or depression from 36.4 per cent to 41.5 per cent, with the fraction reporting unmet mental health care needs increasing from 9.2 per cent to 11.7 per cent. Among children and adolescents, the proportion of mental health–related emergency department visits for those aged 5 to 11 years and 12 to 17 years increased 24 per cent and 31 per cent, respectively, compared with 2019.'

I think a similar pattern is likely in countries around the world.

Analyzing intersections to find positive and dystopian effects

Like any good futures designer / strategic thinker, I find that things get interesting at the intersection of areas. In more in-depth futures work, things are not as easily stated as this Venn diagram (*Fig 4.1*, p.108), so I'm using it as a warm-up to the work that is enabled by the Positive-Dystopian Framework.

---

[50] Helen Pidd, 'Psychosis cases rise in England as pandemic hits mental health', 2021, *Guardian*

[51] Alison M. Darcy and Timothy Mariano, 'Mental Health in America: A Growing Crisis', 2021, *Psychiatric Times*

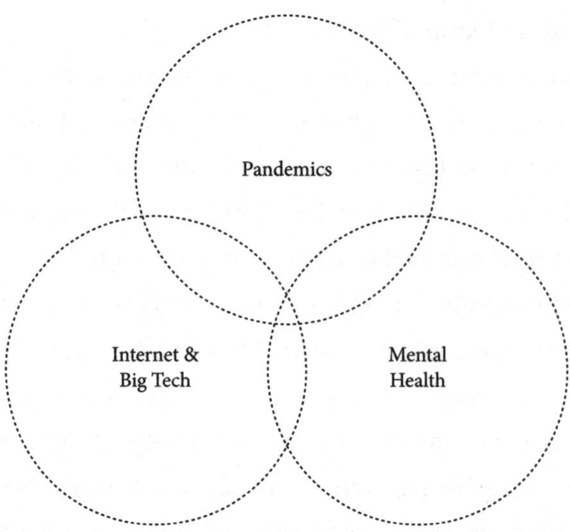

Fig 4.1 The intersection of Pandemics, Internet & Big Tech and Mental Health

We've highlighted several signals in this chapter, and now we can start to wonder what trends we might find at these intersections from positive and dystopian perspectives.

Here are some of my speculations, and feel free to add your own thoughts:

- **Pandemics / Internet & Big Tech**
  - **Positive effects** – the ability to have more effective track and trace activities, better communications regarding therapeutics, remote work capabilities to ensure continuity of business, the ability to collate data to help with research that has informed psychology and therapeutic fields of study.
  - **Dystopian effects** – algorithms take advantage of increased online usage for targeted advertising (and more nefarious activities), increased use of surveillance mechanisms, accelerated burnout and tiredness from using screens for longer periods of times, the erosion of friendships and work relationships etc.

- **Pandemics / Mental Health**
  - **Positive effects** – it seems like a stretch that we find a lot of positives at this intersection, but the increase in business for therapists, an upside in sales for pharmaceutical companies for SSRIs, increased sales of cannabis products certainly benefit a certain segment of society.
  - **Dystopian effects** – these are numerous with increased stress, anxiety, narcissism, loneliness, psychosis, the worsening of other existing conditions, the use of coping mechanisms (alcohol, non-prescription drugs), and even increased suicide.
- **Internet & Big Tech / Mental Health**
  - **Positive effects** – data collection and next best action mechanisms (and identification of at-risk individuals), the facilitation of online counselling/ doctor visits, applications that help with tracking mental health, wearables that help motivate more downtime and physical exercise etc.
  - **Dystopian effects** – data collection, surveillance of individuals, and use of that data to coerce individuals online by government, corporate entities and bad actors.

And, beyond this we can consider the intersection of all three: Pandemics / Internet & Big Tech / Mental Health. Here the interrelationships become more complex and societally apparent. There are also more hidden parts to these relationships, which we must work harder to uncover through foresight work.

The positive effects come together to deliver the ability to really start to make a difference, but the dystopian effects exacerbate the negative effects and directly play against the good that can be done.

This activity is also completely subjective, based on my quick thoughts, and you may feel that there are things missing, and that some have been incorrectly categorized. The problem today is that even such a simple activity is not undertaken by those organizations and governments making decisions. They are caught in a cycle of reaction and quick, ill-considered decision-making influenced by populist stances.

Our dystopian futures?

We can simplify things further by thinking of challenging times ahead by using short-statement stories that are playful and terrifying in the way they are formulated. They are dystopian – raw and visceral to provoke reaction.

I've used short-statement stories to encourage clients to engage with the keynotes I give, and the signals and trends by using a brief 'Future Headline Exercise' – excellent for times when there is a lack of time or a large amount of people with which to do futures work. In this we quickly take trends and imagine the organization's future linked to a year – I typically aim for 10+ years ahead of today.

For the book I asked Bronwyn Williams of Flex Trends in Johannesburg, a friend, futurist and Futurist Think Tank member, to help me brainstorm a few dystopian scenarios and imagine what we might expect to see in the 2040s across several areas.

What resulted was both very amusing (humour is actually a useful tool in futures design) and concerning:

Politics

- President Mark Zuckerberg.
- Europe opts out of the future. Becomes a no-tech zone enclosed in a monumentally large faraday cage. The population has forgotten what the Internet was.
- Democracy isn't working. So, we're doing monarchy and feudalism again.

- Teenage influencer presidents are taking over politics and working on 'gut feel' and memes to guide policy and decision-making, and there's a new term to describe this: 'a memocracy'.

Finance

- The absolute collapse of cryptocurrencies and rise of precious metal and gemstone payments in ghettoized megacities.
- The EU goes bankrupt and becomes a colony of the New Chinese Silk Road Empire.
- The 2034 quantum crypto heists and global digital ecosystem destructors.
- The lights go out – massive solar flare takes out the entire internet. All digital records get fried or scrambled. All debts are void, all identities are lost. It's the greatest reset. Paper bitcoin wallet holders are quite happy, though.
- No microchip, no Universal Basic Income (UBI).

Climate and the water-energy-food nexus

- It's 2050 and the Amazon is stocked with 80 per cent of its fish life as robotic equivalents supplied by the Brazilian government to make people feel like everything is normal. Unfortunately, the cyber-piranhas go berserk due to a software upgrade and kill 25 tourists in 6 hours.
- The golf course agricultural rebellion begins – guerilla food production on the 16th hole and the eventual outlawing of golf as a pastime.
- China and Russia (the 'dragonbear') unite to form the Hot War Axis alliance and engage in activity designed to deliberately warm the planet to take advantage of Arctic trade and oil routes, and farming opportunities.

Wellness and medicine

- Genetic engineering is permitted, but all individuals with an IQ of over 130 or under 100 are forcibly sterilized. Genetic privilege is the issue defining political campaigns.
- Forced mass mind control programmes (chemical lobotomies) become common practice for thought criminals. Social harmony for the greater good justifies this action.
- Babies are born with a 'genetic selection' debt and are expected to repay society. Antenatal genetic engineering debt relief is the new student debt relief – a political hot potato.

High Tech

- The metaverse homeless – game abductors, thieves and hijackers.
- The billionaire elites own all the physical land, live in luxury and force everyone else to farm digital gold in VR headsets while their physical bodies are locked in pod-like cages.
- Transhumanism isn't going so well. Future humans and our robot overlords don't see the point in maintaining mind uploads and cryogenics facilities for billions of millennials (that generation was the *worst*). They are taken offline. Death is a thing again.

Food

- Global supply chain held ransom via a million-strong cypher-criminals hired by local communities, which share in the wealth (like the Somali pirate microeconomics).
- The genetic idealists – perfect children, food, pets and ecosystem. Pay-walled offshore micro civilizations where sex is outlawed, and procreation is by the central administration.

Work, family and communities

- Expressions of happiness outlawed outside of the 'ecstatic hour' of 5–6 p.m. – and the rise of the 'happiness underground'.
- The techno-saviours – the secular churches of Musk and Bezos are established with hundreds of millions of followers globally.
- The last nomad workers – no more global freedom to travel, with people manufacturing their refugee status to be able to live an influencer nomad lifestyle.
- The inhabitants of a fledgling Mars colony – Musk City X15 – synchronously go mad and consume each other when food runs out. The last inhabitant walks out towards the El Dorado dune field, never to be seen again.

These might seem completely outlandish and unlikely to happen – or so it's easy to think. Bronwyn and I could walk through each one and point to signals that indicate a trajectory which could lead us to these scenarios from our standpoint of today.

This is a crude display of what we really need to be doing with futures design / foresight. Looking at dystopian futures, and to the inverse of these positive futures. We invite everyone to imagine the inverse of each scenario as a warm-up exercise prior to the discussion of the Positive-Dystopian Framework overview and example.

CHAPTER FIVE

FACING OUR FUTURES

Broadening our exploration, to include both positive and dystopian futures, leads to greater understanding of how our futures will play out and affect us all.

Remember to imagine and craft the worlds you cannot live without, just as you dismantle the ones you cannot live within.

Ruha Benjamin

Oftentimes we ask, *What do we expect to see wrought on this world in our lifetimes?* We need to disrupt that and ask, *How can we set up the world for success for the next 500 years?* We need to disrupt short-termism and install long-term thinking – as we have discussed previously. By doing so, we gain resiliency, sustainability and the ability to thrive going into our continuous futures. In practical foresight we look at horizons that are a little closer – 10, 20 and 30+ years. Horizons that provide a practical reference point because they are close enough to consider them possible.

There are always positive and dystopian signals, trends, pathways and trajectories that carry us into our futures. These are philosophical human concepts that are contextual and uncover our motivations and worldview.

I've always said that we need to consider positive and dystopian trajectories. What we see is that executives and political leaders often posit that positive mindsets alone are the only way to truly be the most successful. Yes, positive energy is a powerful driving force. However, through the work I have undertaken with my clients, I understand that organizations will go much deeper into the work of designing futures when they have a clear idea of dystopian scenarios – what can go wrong, how ideas can be hijacked for nefarious purposes, and the domino effects across geopolitics and society.

Over the past 10+ years in researching, producing events, advising and teaching clients about the application of foresight, I have gained the ability to embrace both positive and dystopian futures. My event DARK FUTURES was certainly a catalyst for this because the speakers invited spoke about the hidden systems and dystopian effects that they themselves have caused.

A side effect of this was that I am often perceived as not being wholly optimistic – especially after my keynotes, which can be overwhelming for audience members forced to consider the potential disruption to their industries and lives.

I need to set things straight. I am overwhelmingly positive and optimistic, and yet I am not afraid to investigate the darkness and consider the dynamics of dystopian futures. This keeps my thoughts sober and my eyes wide open on how those ideas of positive futures can be affected by dystopian effects and trajectories. Through hundreds of hours of working with clients and thousands of hours of research over the years, I have developed a framework and method that helps me. I am now sharing this to add to the processes and methods that are already in the world and being used each day to expand our thinking on our futures.

It's called the *Positive-Dystopian Futures Framework* and draws inspiration from several methods I have mentioned in this book – namely Dator's 4 Futures and the Futures Cone, and it draws on the experience I have gleaned through 25 years of strategic consulting using tools like PESTLE, STEEP – and their derivatives, including the Business Model Canvas – informing product and organizational roadmaps.

This method has come together through trial and error. From complex ideas and cognitive exercises. From experimentation on the job, and through seeing clients transform how they approach the visions, principles and strategies that drive their organizations to do more every day.

This section covers several areas relating to the Positive-Dystopian Futures Framework, and the next chapter will take us through a working example with a modern context.

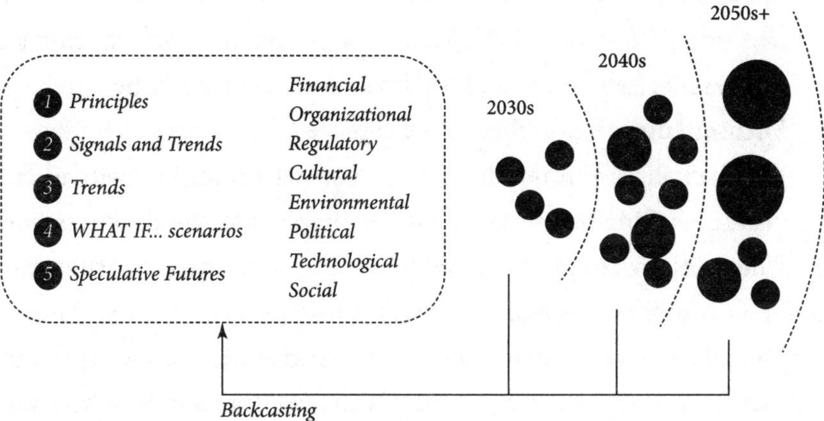

Fig 5.1 Positive-Dystopian Futures Framework, Conceptual View. Copyright Nikolas Badminton, 2021

The framework can be read from left to right with the following elements

- **Principles** – the foundational positive and dystopian principles that we follow through the process and which guide our exploration and thinking.

- **Signals and Trends** – the signals of change that we scan for, and the trends that emerge from several of those signals converging.
- **What if… scenarios** – the hypothetical scenarios that we present as short stories to create succinct narratives on our futures relating to trends and signals and framed by the positive and dystopian principles.
- **Dimensions for consideration** – the Financial, Organizational, Regulatory, Cultural, Environmental, Political, Technological and Social dimensions can all be explored and their effects identified. Together these conveniently spell FORCEPTS – a play on the word *forceps*, helping us to grasp, retract or stabilize ideas on our futures.
- **Speculative Futures** – those explorations of what our futures could be through the means of speculative fiction and the experiential futures that help us see and feel how the futures might be.
- **Futures Initiatives** – these are the projects, policies and actions – the black circles in the diagram – that can be seen as needed for progression in the time horizons. These speculations allow us to see what initiative might be needed in our futures and can span some or all combinations and areas of FORCEPTS.
- **10 / 20 / 30+ year horizons** – the timeframe periods we set out in which to root the scenarios we outline for our futures. I typically use 10 / 20 / 30+ year horizons because they are far enough in our futures not to be wholly attainable today using our current ways of working and systems in place, and 10 years is close enough to have hope that we are able to start making progress towards designing our possible futures. Be warned, it's tempting to bring the horizons closer to make more impact, so resolve to keep them longer term.

The process we follow through the framework, and detail behind each step is explained as follows…

Framing our motivations

Why do we even need to consider our futures?

I've heard this many times as I speak to organizations and individuals that are very much focused on the now and near future. However, the SARS-CoV-2 (Covid-19) pandemic has really awakened the amount of interest in considering future horizons because its effects have been felt so deeply in every part of society. The clients who have approached me and my team have been varied – trillion-dollar tech companies with global operations, central banks, governments, property developers, international recruiters, municipalities and urban planners, banks and insurance companies, and news media companies.

Each one of them realized that their strategic planning – typically with a view out to between 18 and 36 months – was leaving them unprepared for disruption and unforeseen risks such as those we've seen in the pandemic – including remote work and team collaboration, supply chain issues, food supply, changes in climate impact and mental health. It has also accelerated the consideration of several technologies, such as robotic process automation (RPA), remote collaboration tools, virtual reality, the rise of the metaverse as a dominant narrative, and the redesign of collaborative environments in-office. The impending restructuring of power dynamics in society like this is a good motivator for organizations to start undertaking foresight work.

The period from 2020 through to 2022 felt like a 20-month boot camp for the Futurist Think Tank, with organizations trying to make sense of their place in an ever-changing world and new foresight practices. It also turns out there were more areas than I could've imagined which I had to go deep into for my clients during and following the pandemic:

- The risk of new zoonotic diseases entering society
- New health protocols and biomedical preparedness
- Climate change (it is not healing and will likely get worse)
- Drought, famine and locust plagues
- The end of oil and gas as dominant fuels and funding of fossil fuel exploration entirely
- Technology infrastructure impact
- Virtual engagement and tactical user experience
- Wearable computing
- Addiction and mental health
- The future of collaborative and nomadic work
- Urbanization, and the design of the city and office
- Sustainable construction
- Food systems and supply chain
- Civil unrest, organized crime, private militias and cybercrime
- The impact of 'defunding the police'

I officially became the worst person to chat to about the pandemic in the bar. On the flipside, the signals and thinking became invaluable to organizations trying to work out what comes next. One common theme is shared – our futures have never been convenient, and now more people are understanding that in a very real and visceral way.

The pandemic has felt, and continues to feel, like it has created a perfect space in which to explore the value of foresight for the organization. We're in a constant cycle of knowing where we are and then finding that being disrupted quickly – by new variants, market dynamics, inflation and other effects. Executives need better references on possible futures and the dynamics within them to create resiliency in their organizations.

Who decides what positive futures and dystopian futures are?

While writing this book I spent time in California, and I managed to catch up with several people to discuss this project and the ideas and structures of the Positive-Dystopian Framework. I had decided on what I considered what positive futures are and how dystopian futures could play out.

One of these was Heather Vescent, up in Joshua Tree, California, and we had a chance to discuss why we need more positive futures planning. She challenged me to look at dystopian futures as well. She also said something quite pertinent:

> 'Who gets to decide what is positive and what is dystopian?'

That really resonated with me, and I began to think a lot about my personal stance on this and the experience, worldview, hopes and biases that inform those definitions. I also realized that it is important to have open and clear discussions within organizations on their goals, and with the people who are the decision-makers, to understand their moral beliefs, ethical stances and biases.

For the Positive-Dystopian Framework to be useful and result in more equitable and positive futures, we must be clear about what this means. Or else, people could flip definitions on their heads and apply their thinking in ways that the framework is trying to avoid – think about oil companies saying positive futures need extensive heavy industry infrastructure powered by 'clean fossil fuels', and that dystopia is the inability to provide alternative energy and means.

Here are the definitions of positive and dystopian futures I use to guide how we use the Positive-Dystopian Framework:

Positive Futures – a world where we have a global view, and infrastructure to support, improving health and wellness, and reducing wealth disparity. A world where we design humanity-centric, balanced and egalitarian solutions to our greatest challenges. A world where we rely on a reduced reliance on the few companies that want to change the world and towards an empowerment of every person on the planet to have ownership of their own identity (and their data), and a right to exist with their hopes, dreams and opinions in any place in our world, and in our futures. A world where we see infinite futures and plan for them accordingly through the application of positive principles of change. And, ultimately, a world where wars are no more, and any conflict can be resolved through rational discussion and collaboration.

Dystopian Futures – a world where we perpetuate the reliance on the industrial complex, supported by military action and conflict, and where billionaires and shareholders are rewarded ahead of any of the users of technology solutions/platforms. A world that is led by short-term thinking and greed, and where personal protectionism is apparent and unashamed. A world where leadership ego is left unchecked and short-term effects are rewarded. A world of corporate and governmental surveillance and control to ensure we all have futures that fall in line with the visions of the few people that want to shape the singular future.

Positive Futures design looks at the possible, plausible and probable futures we would like to see play out over the next 10, 20 and 30+ years. A world where anything is possible – as encouraged by both technocrats and politicians. Yet it's a world that very often has little rigour in planning. The Positive-Dystopian Futures Framework aims to introduce that rigour to these conversations while supporting a positive view. However, this cannot be the whole story.

That's where the other side of things, Dystopian Futures design, comes into play. I always say that our futures are terribly inconvenient. They have the potential to disrupt existing situations or strengthen power and control for the few while so many are caught in the cultural and technological web of the industrial complex. This is where we flex our futures design muscles with the idea of Preposterous Futures, as discussed in Chapter 1.

And this approach enables us to identify the unforeseen risks, activities that we need to carefully consider and plan, and indicators of where we need to engage multiple parties to ensure we have a resilient path to our futures.

Positive-Dystopian Framework process

The flow of futures design – for both positive and dystopian futures – has 10 distinct steps if we follow it in its entirety. Steps 1 to 8 are the minimum, and Steps 9 (Backcasting) and 10 (Strategic Planning) are additional steps that we recommend teams follow to help bring futures narratives and the relevancy of signals and trends, and their long-term effects, back to the discussions around strategic planning today.

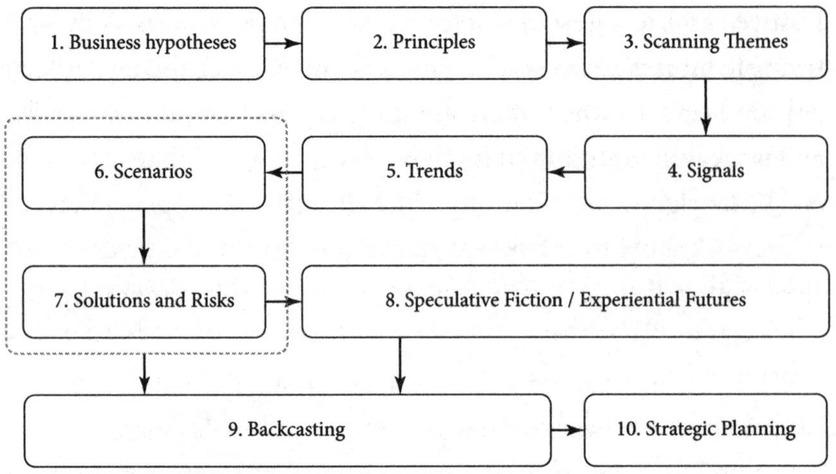

Fig 5.2 Positive-Dystopian Framework Process Flow

Step 1: Write the Business Hypotheses and Set the Horizons

We typically frame the work by outlining one to three hypotheses that we could be facing in our futures – business disruptions, societal tensions, war, climate change, mental health etc.

As a rule of thumb, we set the target horizon for envisaging futures closer to the present day, depending on the organization's comfort with futures work and/or their willingness to play with our futures.

> *Note: there are some organizations that default to longer views – for example, airlines, airports, large infrastructure developers, engineering companies – so I tend to always start at 30+ years out and use 100 years as a far horizon. The nice thing I've found in developing and using this framework is that it is completely flexible – as all good frameworks should be. Rigidity makes it difficult to progress, particularly in large organizations.*

I use SMART as a guide for setting out my problem areas – I've been trying to limit the acronyms as much as possible, but we can see them pop up in places where it's useful to apply them. These are adapted and work well for futures design:

Specific – target a specific area or capability for improvement and its related actors, processes, governance, data practices, cultural elements, providers and consumers.
Measurable – we should always choose something that is quantifiable, or which has a way to gauge progress through narrative and impacts on people, processes and systems.
Assignable – we need to specify those affected in broad and specific senses. This is incredibly important because these are the actors who will be affected in the futures we design.
Realistic – in strategic planning this is about stating what results we can expect, which helps in determining return on investment (ROI), budgets and resource planning. In futures planning it is blue sky and speculative. We can really build out bigger goals against the idea of a future state; we should set no limits when undertaking futures work.
Time-related – instead of specifying when the results can be achieved, we can state where we want progress to be at each of the horizons we set at the beginning of the work.

In addition to applying SMART to frame our work, we need to set a core hypothesis. A hypothesis will help us state our starting ideas on the futures we hope to create and outlines what we hope to find as we research signals and identify trends.

It's typical to start a project with a certain level of understanding, and we can base our hypothesis on that. When entering a net new area of investigation, it is important to do an initial scan of signals and potential trends at this stage. Remember, a hypothesis is not just a guess but should be based on existing theories and knowledge – essential when we are undertaking futures work.

An example set of hypotheses, framed in a statement, is:

> As the global population grows to 9.6 billion people in 2050, the world will need to produce 60 per cent more food, and we will need a more productive and resilient agriculture and supply chain ecosystem – especially in cities.

We've stated growth (population), a basic need (more food production), identified systemic elements (resilient agriculture and supply chain ecosystem) and provided a specific target group (city dwellers). It's a mirror from which we reflect ideas of our futures.

We then set our horizons. The horizons we typically focus on are the 2030s, 2040s, 2050s – and beyond. The 2030s are close enough to feel like the work will have relevancy and the 2040s and 2050s far enough away to ensure we are focused on futures exploration. We always recommend rooting the work we do at the middle horizon, as it lets us establish a baseline and then take a step forward to think about wilder ideas, and a step back to allow us to see the linkages from today to those futures.

Step 2: Set Foundational Principles

Foundational principles provide the framing, rules and guidelines that serve as a reference for thinking about the longer-term of our organization, how it plays in existing and new industries, and how it will be an active participant in shaping our future in the world. When considered carefully and applied properly, they will help ensure that the team understand the futures that we are trying to explore.

They will also give direction for the organization, focus our futures planning efforts, eliminate distractions while still considering them, and set a number of priorities when creating a longer-term view. They can also help organizations define measures of success for our futures.

Here are the rules we follow when setting principles:

- Apply SMART principles.
- Consider practices and behaviours.
- Remove ambiguity.
- Be visionary and impactful, and don't be afraid of upsetting your comfort and pushing the boundaries of what you are doing today.

At this stage we double our efforts to state both positive and dystopian principles as sounding boards for when we analyze signals, identify trends and then develop the scenarios to identify the opportunities and business risks.

An example of a positive future principle is:

> Consider solutions from the perspective of human needs, not technological capability.

That means we ground the work in human needs – certainty, variety, significance, connection and love, growth and contribution – and not from the potential lock-in to certain functionalities of a technological platform which means we can do things only in the way the platform provider lets us via rigid functionalities.

On the flipside, an example of a reflective dystopian future principle is:

> Consider solutions from a technological capability perspective, with human needs as secondary and inconvenient.

That means we look for solutions which best fit what we need rather than redesigning from the ground up. That's a recipe for technological colonization and restrictive application, and the ownership of data and actions within that platform. Sounds quite familiar in today's high-tech world where data is the world's most important resource.

Step 3: Scanning Themes

With the principles in place and a well-thought-through business hypothesis, we can start with a list of scanning themes / areas of interest to explore as we start to scan for signals. Example themes could be food prices and logistics, global shifts on population and city growth, impacts of climate change, changing energy landscape, water scarcity and other areas.

It's very likely that these may broaden or come together as composite areas as we progress through the exercise. This is fine and an expected part of the process. It's important for the team to note what caused the focus to change because it may provide useful reference as we progress through the work.

Step 4: Signals

Signals are distinct pieces of information, technologies and digital infrastructure, geopolitical movements, cultural shifts, statistics, stories, activities and/or events that indicate an impending shift or change or an emerging issue that may become significant in our futures.

We need to undertake focused research and look for both weak and strong signs that indicate how the trajectory across culture, government and technologies is changing. It's typical for secondary research – i.e. the collation, summary and/or synthesis of existing research – to lead this effort because it's faster to tap into online sources of information. It also allows us to create links across many signals, which leads to deeper considerations of what the signals mean.

Primary research – the creation of insights through surveys, interviews, in-depth observation of behaviours – can play a role, although it can hinder the process because it always brings us back to the now. We recommend starting with secondary research and, if required, beginning the primary research elements at the same time while ensuring that the problem statement and hypotheses are well understood and shared.

The process we follow to find good signals is as follows…

First review the hypothesis, areas of interest and themes, and hold them in mind when scanning for signals

Scanning is a daily task for the team. We are constantly looking out for reference points and the signals of change in real life and in articles, videos, documentaries, podcasts, academic research, and other futures studies publications. There are several ways to do this efficiently. We connect with and follow notable thinkers on social media – especially through Twitter and now TikTok – and follow their publications. I also follow several keywords relating to the futures I am designing and search for news each day. Google Alerts can help with this, although it can get tedious over time to receive so many emails. For a few years now we have followed and been active participants in Reddit's /r/futurology subreddit. That is a great point of reference to find new developments and see the discussions because there are over 15.7 million members. There is also a lot of noise, though, so be aware of that.

It is important to consider scanning outside of the 'tech bubble' as well because there are important insights out in the community – at events with people who provide support and services for our lives, and in government discussions.

It is always good to allow several weeks for the scanning process so that we can create a long list of signals and consider them across themes. For each signal, summarize the title of the work, source, key insights and the potential implications on our futures. We actively share early scanning with the client and then invite them to live with the signals and not rush the process. We need time for consideration. Typically, we enforce a five- to ten-day gap between discussing the signals and trends prior to developing scenarios and holding workshops. Organizations do like to move quickly, so we warn that making faster decisions could mean missing some important considerations.

As we find more signals, they will change our perspective on others that we have already found. Discuss these with team members and select significant ones to share, especially if they can have a marked impact today. I truly believe that if we are doing futures work properly, it is OK for some parts of futures work to resonate today. However, there is a caveat.

> Do not use the signals, and their intersections, we find to make quick decisions. This can lead to problems down the line because this is typically planned and executed tactically, and the ramifications of actions taken quickly are not considered with a full view of internal and external factors.

Once we have let some time pass, and have reviewed the scanning, we can find several signals seem to stand out from the list, so reduce to a short list of impactful signals. I typically find 20 to 30 signals to be a useful number to consider when designing futures, because we are going to search for more as we continue the process. Also, group these signals into broader themes and areas of interest. That helps us when identifying trends.

Then we can consider the positive and dystopian effects of each. This is the creative part and where we will need to discuss with people what might happen speculatively.

Note: This is a core part of the Positive-Dystopian Futures process because signals can have positive and dystopian effects. For each, or for each grouping of signals, we outline those effects as they are inherited by the trends we will identify.

For example, we might have a signal that states that 'there will be explosive growth in the populations of Asia and even more so in Africa, especially in megacities, from 2022 to 2100'. We might then consider this in relation to our hypotheses and speculate as follows:

- **Positive effects** – growth of urban populations leads to growing economies and new opportunities for trade and the provision of food and medicine; the creation of new models of business for megacities and communities growing their own food; and so on.
- **Dystopian effects** – reduced access to food, the prevalence of food black markets and underground dealing; the increased possibility of widespread foodborne illness; an increased need in healthcare, increasing mortality rates due to malnutrition; and so on.

Step 5: Identifying Trends

A trend is a general direction in which something is developing or changing, and is created by existing conditions and environments, and is affected by one or more signals.

After scanning for signals and ascertaining the positive and dystopian effects, identifying trends is one of the most important tasks when undertaking foresight. By doing so we allow ourselves to create a basis for our decisions and the scenarios we explore. It creates urgency and a sense of realism about where we are headed.

It's usual to group one or more signals together to uncover even more speculative trends and then to combine trends into broader megatrends that have a wider, and potentially, global impact.

It helps to group trends at different levels:

- **Megatrends** – typically these are long-term developments over several decades that have a formative effect on all areas of society and the economy worldwide – such as the interplay of geopolitics and the water-food-energy nexus, pandemics, state-sponsored cyberattacks etc. These are usual for broader considerations but are not necessarily useful for writing detailed scenarios, so do not focus exclusively on these.
- **System trends** – these are the trends that are seen across the use of systems in the real world, such as the application of machine learning, the growth of data, shifts in large social media platforms etc. It is likely that most trends we will find are system trends. Be careful. Too many of these will make the scenarios we build overly systematic – no surprise there – and we need to ensure that we come back to our principles, which should put humanity ahead of technology. Consider human and community behaviours in relation to the systems that we may see. It will create a larger view of our futures.

- **Localized and individual trends** – these are typified by those that have immediate impact on an organization in a particular market, or in a particular locale. And individual trends relate to individuals, groups or communities of people. Typically, direct impact is felt more immediately with these trends and discussed extensively in these places. Localized and individual trends will play against system trends and be influenced by megatrends.

There will need to be time for reflection following the identification of trends. At this point, cluster trends in themes that will play a role in the scenarios, assess their relevance to the organization and the scope of their impact, and the time periods in which we may see their acceleration and impact (the short to medium term). We may also choose to prioritize trends, which is useful if we end up with a longer list than expected. For example, we may choose the Top 5 trends out of a longer list of 15. Do not completely disregard the other trends we set aside; we may find it interesting to revisit them as we build out scenarios.

At this stage we might feel our futures worldview to be getting richer, and now is a good time to stop and reflect on what might happen in our broader industry and world futures. That's useful in priming us for the next part of the process.

Step 7: Developing What If… scenarios, and Identifying Solutions and Risks

We've already discussed shifting our mindsets from what is to what if… It's an invitation to be curious, and we can use What If… scenarios to help us to create quick, short stories of possible actions or events in the future. These are short, statement-based stories that present future states and provide the canvas for exploring specific areas.

Building scenarios is more intensive in terms of work. We need to take the signals, the positive and dystopian effects, and the trends that are identified from them and then consider impacts across several dimensions.

At this stage we state the trends that we are using for the scenario – I typically choose three, which allows for some complexity without being too overbearing for our creative thinking. We then collect the positive and dystopian effects which become *opportunities* (positive) and *risks* (dystopian). That nomenclature works better for the writing of scenarios and allows us to integrate positive and dystopian effects.

We then brainstorm what speculative solutions could exist, and we state a time in which to state the scenarios. As I've mentioned, the horizons we typically focus on are the 2030s, 2040s, 2050s – and beyond. We often focus on the 2040s because this allows us to suspend disbelief and imagine the futures that may come to pass.

As we progress through the process, we can look ahead to the 2050s and also step back to the 2030s to speculate from there about the path forwards, and the interim steps that we may see ahead of us from today. We will then also undertake backcasting using speculative solutions and anticipated risks from the 2040s. More on that later (page 141).

There are two parts we typically follow to build out scenarios, which is about the distillation of ideas to create more succinct scenarios:

Part One – take three of the trends that seem to be of high interest to our organization, then take the signals that feed into them, and identify opportunities and challenges from the positive and dystopian effects that have been identified. We can then create a list of 3 to 5 speculative solutions that could serve these trends. This provides a comprehensive view that can be discussed prior to reducing to succinct scenarios in the next two steps.

Part Two – take three solutions, identify the business opportunities and risks, and then explore impacts across several dimensions of change.

By doing so, we are able structure our thinking into a What if… scenario:

What if in the [2040s]
solutions
[a, b, and c are implemented],
which creates these
[opportunities and risks],
and impacts
[dimensions of change]

As part of the scenario building and backcasting, we build out a list of influencing factors across the following dimensions: Financial, Organizational, Regulatory, Cultural, Environmental, Political, Technological, and Social – FORCEPTS, as mentioned earlier. I always think every framework needs a good acronym that plays on the intent and leads to memorization, so I use FORCEPTS in this work. It seems apt because we are holding and grasping at ideas and, in a way, birthing futures, much like forceps help doctors to do. Here are the boundaries of each of the dimensions that we typically explore:

Financial (and Economic) factors include levels of investment in legacy, planned and new projects, subsidies, economic movements of growth and decline, and exchange / inflation / interest rates, inflation, availability of jobs, the start-up ecosystem and entrepreneurship. We can also consider the Total Addressable Market (TAM), Total Cost of Ownership (TCO) and the investment needed for customer engagement, legacy systems maintenance and migration.

Organizational factors include cultural values, departmental responsibilities and reporting hierarchies, board-level involvement, C-suite structure and accountability, organizational structures, communications perforation, innovation, futures planning capabilities (if any) and strategic planning integration across departments in the organization. In addition, we can consider the dynamics of how people behave and react to each other, and of how the organization can be made to work more effectively.

Regulatory (and Legal) factors include local government by-laws, federal and state laws and associated regulations, international and national standards, securities regulations, and mechanisms to monitor and ensure compliance with these. We can also consider discrimination law, consumer law, antitrust law, employment law, and health and safety law. An example of a regulatory factor is a decision made that contravenes local laws to progress new business models – something we've seen a lot of from the ride-hailing industry where they are willing to pay fines and skirt laws to gain new customers and encourage usage.

Cultural factors relate to simple and complex patterns of human activity and the symbolic structures that give such activities significance and importance. We must consider both company culture

– how the people in an organization bond and agree on intention and purpose – and society at large in relation to events, customs, group / community / regional / country identity, the arts, social institutions, and the achievements of a particular nation, people or other social group. An example of a cultural factor is tensions between factors in a community on civic issues relating to community representation and development.

Environmental factors involve ecological and environmental aspects such as water, soil, wind, energy, food, climate change and pollution, and regulations relating to environmental monitoring and control for industries. We need to consider the need to grow awareness and more deeply understand the potential impacts of climate change and how that is affecting how companies operate and the products and services they offer – in legacy businesses, when considering the creation of new markets, or disrupting (and potentially destroying) existing ones. An example of an environmental factor is local emissions in relation to heavy industries, or the carbon footprint of business travel and operations for clients and others in their industry.

Political factors relate to how the government entities intervene in the local, state and federal economy. Governments, and the political wrangling within, have a high impact on the togetherness, infrastructure, health and education of a nation. Political factors may also include goods and services which the government aims to provide or be provided – also known as merit goods – and those that the government does not want to be provided – also known as demerit goods. It is important to be aware of likely upcoming shifts in power and the political conversations and debates around critical factors. These can highly influence organizations and individuals, and affect financial markets, trade, antitrust, environmental and other kinds of laws. An example of a political factor are the promises made on the campaign trail of winning candidates for political positions of power that look short term within the next electoral cycle without considerations of longer-term futures.

Technological factors include the transformation of technological infrastructure – Internet, hardware and software, patents and intellectual property, research and development (R & D) that drives innovation, robotic process automation and applications of machine learning (sometimes more broadly referred to as Artificial Intelligence), technology incentives, and the rate of technological change, exponential or otherwise. Other factors can include energy usage, transport, patent regulations and life cycle of products. An example of a technological factor is the adoption of technological frameworks and standards for the storage and encryption of data using cryptographic technologies.

Social factors include consumer behaviour demographics, religion, lifestyles, values, advertising, community cohesion, health consciousness, population growth rate, age distribution, career attitudes and emphasis on safety. High trends in social factors affect the demand for a company's products and how that company operates. An example of a social factor is an ageing population, and an independent-minded younger workforce may imply a smaller pool of people to feed local industries, thus increasing the cost of labour.

These present the opportunity to do a great deal of speculative work when building our rich scenarios. In practical terms I recommend a focus on brainstorming factors that provide colour and complex dynamics upfront – Organizational, Cultural, Environmental and Technological.

When backcasting and considering current strategic planning, we revisit the remaining factors – Financial, Regulatory, Political, and Social – as a group. The scenarios will have enough information and complexity to better discuss them.

Of course, we can look at FORCEPTS holistically from the get-go. However, this can prove to be overwhelming with a working group that is also learning about futures design, identifying trends, spelling out positive and dystopian effects, and building scenarios.

For Part Two of the process, we recommend taking three solutions, and identifying the business opportunities and risks, and exploring impacts across Organizational, Cultural, Environmental, and Technological development. We then structure them into a What if… scenario, as follows:

What if in the [2040s]
solutions
[a, b, and c are implemented],
which creates these
[opportunities and risks],
and impacts
[Organizational, Cultural, Environmental, and Technological development].

The most effective foresight work will generate several scenarios, and these feed into the vision of a world at those future horizons. As a guide I suggest a minimum of five well-considered scenarios. It is also a fantastic idea to present the scenarios we have to other people or groups and allow discussion and questions, which often means that additional ideas are surfaced.

Exploring our horizons

We can take a higher-level view of what we may expect to experience and see in these horizons. If our scenario is rooted in the 2040s, take these ideas and speculate briefly – by thinking about the evolution of their dynamics into the 2050s – and how they will become dominant over time, and the internal and external factors that could affect them. We can then switch our thoughts to the 2030s and then think about the interim steps – between today and that horizon – which can lead towards those futures.

Looking back can be further explored in a collaborative setting using the steps for backcasting and strategic planning – this will be discussed in more detail in Chapter 8.

Once we have worked through each stage together, these futures should all feel possible with empowerment of communities and a balance that creates a more equitable world. It's inevitable that some legacy businesses and individuals unwilling to adapt will become obsolete. Unfortunately, that has become the natural cycle of things for many organizations, and we need to question the role and motivation of those resistant to change and how we want to create resiliency.

We remind clients that change itself is, in fact, the only thing that is certain. We can either open ourselves to positive change and see those challenges, or we can refuse and lock ourselves into a cycle that will, by design, lead us along a dystopian trajectory accelerated by ignorance.

Step 8: Speculative Fiction and Experiential Futures

Speculative fiction is the approach of writing fictional stories or creating visual elements that tell a story. These are typically an evolution of the scenarios we've developed with expressions of future artefacts, recorded history, nature or the present universe. Speculative fiction includes Design fiction (short stories), Longer-form fiction (books and whitepapers), poetry and other literary devices, short videos and art. *Experiential futures* expand to include something we can touch, hear, walk through and/or immerse ourselves in. Both forms may take people into supernatural and other imaginative realms. These usually take the form of installations and sculpture, video and various multimedia.

We explore these ideas further in Chapter 7: Igniting Imagination.

Steps 9 and 10: Backcasting, and Strategic Considerations

We can follow the Positive-Dystopian Framework process through to Step 8 and provide a great deal of value to the organization. It's a strong first step towards exploring our futures. The question remains: *How do we connect this work back to our strategic thinking and planning today?*

The answer is by following two further steps: Backcasting (Step 9) and Strategic Planning (Step 10).

The steps of Backcasting and Strategic Planning will be discussed in detail in Chapter 8. To ensure we have a complete view of this process, what follows here is a primer to help us understand their role in shaping the organization.

Backcasting allows us to travel backwards from the futures we have created to where we are today by identifying strategic considerations from the futures scenarios we have built; considering what people need to be involved, what processes need to evolve or be installed, what governance (internal and external) is needed, and what solutions need to be put into place; and, outlining the programmes and projects that need to be established and a view on the investments needed and who will help support that journey.

Beyond backcasting mixed with storytelling, we can more directly identify strategic considerations from our scenarios and integrate them into strategic planning. If we scan all the opportunities and risks, then we can start to identify several strategic considerations to be noted as we undertake our existing strategic planning activities.

These considerations can be fed into the strategic planning process today. This is the link from the futures we have designed to help anticipate roadblocks and risks while providing business value through foresight.

Worldbuilding

The Positive-Dystopian Framework allows us to consider what our futures could be and, more importantly, what that world could be like. There's a real value behind all this work and that is to connect the people in the organization to the futures that could lie ahead. There is another part of what we are doing in foresight – we are building our thinking on our futures in a world that is different to today.

This is an activity that all science fiction authors, artists and filmmakers are familiar with, as are we, the audiences consuming those stories. Once we have reached the trends and scenarios stage of our work, we can stop and reflect on the world that we will occupy in those futures and record our thoughts.

While we cannot imagine the futures trajectories of every organization, community, city and country, we can certainly sketch out what world those fictional futures exist within. We can reflect on expected changes in the climate, geography, the environment, the people that live in the places we operate (including our own employees), how government might work, and the technologies that we might rely on. We can also consider more mundane aspects. How does garbage collection work? What will TV programming and media look like? What will people do for fun? And, who supports and services the populace as they go about their daily lives?

We'll explore this further in the next two chapters. In Chapter 6 we will build out an example of working through the Positive-Dystopian Framework by looking at signals and trends relating to global food futures for an organization that wants to create a more sustainable and resilient world where we can feed more people in cities and beyond. Then, in Chapter 7, we will look at the role of speculative fiction and experiential futures.

CHAPTER SIX

GLOBAL WATER-ENERGY-FOOD FUTURES

Working to identify Positive and Dystopian trajectories to identify futures, solutions and risks that lead to a more equitable world, and preferable futures.

Ask the questions that have no answers. Invest in the millennium. Plant sequoias.

Wendell Berry, Manifesto: The Mad Farmer Liberation Front

When working on futures design and foresight, we have a focus on a client and industry. For the example in this chapter, I am choosing agriculture and related areas – water, energy, food production, the supply chain etc.

This is an area in which I've always been interested. I grew up in a farming town in the south-west of England. My father worked in 'protein processing' – aka a slaughterhouse – and then for over 30 years in the wholesale dairy industry. I also worked in the dairy business for three years after school, before going back into education to focus on technology and computing. I was born into an agricultural and agri-food ecosystem, and those memories still live with me today.

I have also worked with significant players in the food industry from a farming, agricultural supply, system, innovation, and agri-food production perspective. In my work, and in this book, I wanted to explore futures design and foresight in these areas. I am drawing on recent consulting experiences with large farming operations (aiming for increasing yields of protein, fruits, vegetables and other crops), agricultural industry players (providers of equipment, fertilizers, data analytic platforms, sensors, precision agriculture and other supporting capabilities) and food producers and providers around the world (from agri-food to food retail and the infrastructure that supports them).

There are two main reasons to choose this industry and its supporting areas for exploration:

- **Impact on a global scale** – agriculture presents some of the most interesting areas to explore due to the impact of production and availability of food for every person on the planet, i.e., food sovereignty, ensuring accessibility to affordable food, mastering the water-energy-food nexus and being on the cutting edge of agricultural technologies.
- **Scalability into our futures** – it was agriculture that helped us humans establish larger settlements and the first large cities and create a surplus of food that created economic wealth and power. We can track this back some 10,000 years ago to cities like Uruk, situated east of the present bed of the Euphrates River in what is now known as Iraq.

For our example I will use a fictitious entity: a well-funded, private investment company based in California, known for their ability to forge new futures in the agricultural (growing food), agri-food (processed and packaged food plus foodservice), pharma crop (crops grown and processed to provide compounds to be used in pharmaceuticals), and plant-based medicine (psychedelics and psychoactive compounds).

Note: No companies, people or situations represented in this example relate to real companies, people or situations that my clients, or their partners, are experiencing. Any similarities are purely coincidental. Real found signals are used throughout the example with references provided in the footnotes to the original sources.

Organization X, an agricultural futures company

Organization X is a three-year-old private investment company that is well funded ($145 billion+) and looking to build out its visions for resilient and sustainable agriculture in the context of megacities and its associated portfolio of solutions that address agriculture resiliency (the water-food-energy nexus and climate-related challenges), in-field agriculture, agri-food systems, local and global food supply chain, and food / nutrition in relation to communities, health, wellness and longevity. Organization X is also actively building partnerships with start-ups, Venture Funds and established companies. They also lobby the US government relating to their areas of interest.

While Organization X has a global focus, they have strategically placed themselves in Menlo Park in California to be close to funding conversations and to study the challenges with the futures state of global climate warming, desertification, water-resilient crops and the effect of continued severe drought. The company is betting on futures where resiliency and sustainability in large-scale food and urban food production are needed, and profitable.

They have a particular interest in creating a new group of companies – an agritech portfolio – to revolutionize and create rigorous agricultural practices, via a research hub for resilient food systems that influences practices in California, North America and global strategic locations, such as Africa and China.

Organization X have approached the Futurist Think Tank to help them scan for signals, create an understanding of trends that are affecting markets and food availability globally, and create scenarios that help them look some 10, 20 and 30+ years into the future. This will help them create futures visions to help influence investments – start-ups to fund and mentor, R & D efforts – and governmental policies, partnerships, and customers to target, starting in California and the adjacent states. They are interested in engaging the Futurist Think Tank to explore their futures using the Positive-Dystopian Framework.

We invite several people to be involved from Organization X to be a part of the team involved in the process of futures design:

- **Futurist Think Tank** – the Chief Futurist to lead and guide the work and act as the project liaison, a Lead Analyst to help source signals and develop candidate trends, and a number of supporting futurists / foresight practitioners to produce the reports and coordinate activities in the workshops and subsequent communications.
- **Organization X** – we invite the chief executives – CEO, CSO, CMO and COO ideally – plus the VP Growth, Head of Green Tech Investments, Creative Director and Key Designers. In addition, the Chairperson and Board Representatives are also invited to be a part of this work and briefed on the outcomes if they do not participate.
- **Industry partners** – Organization X may select a few trusted representatives from their trusted network of advisors, partners, investors, start-ups and most-valued clients.

Positive-Dystopian Futures Framework and Process Flow

The flow of futures design – for both positive and dystopian futures – has 10 distinct steps if we follow it in its entirety – here we provide this as a reference and reminder.

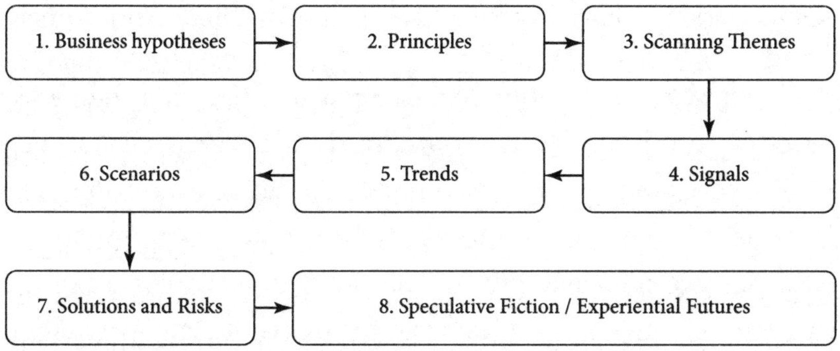

Fig 6.1 Positive-Dystopian Framework Process Flow

Here we walk through a real-world example of the work.

Step 1: Write Business Hypotheses and Set the Horizons

Team Instructions: Define the SMART hypotheses that we will set out to prove to be true or false with the futures we will set out to design.

The hypotheses we will choose to help frame our thinking is:

As the population grows to 9.6 billion people in 2050, the world will need to produce 60 per cent more food, and we will need a more productive and resilient agriculture and supply chain ecosystem – especially in cities.

We also select horizons that we will focus on – the 2030s, 2040s, 2050s and beyond. Our futures design work will focus on the 2040s, which allows for us to suspend disbelief and imagine the futures states that may come to pass. We will then look beyond – to the 2050s – and step back – to the 2030s – to speculate on the path forwards, and the interim steps that we may see ahead of us. We will then also backcast, using speculative solutions and anticipated risks from the 2040s.

Step 2: Set Foundational Principles

Team Instructions: Identify foundational positive and dystopian principles from which we can consider signals, trends and develop scenarios. This is an activity to be completed ahead of any collaborative session and agreed upon by the organization and working group.

Our positive principles provide the ability to imagine a trajectory that drives us towards an ideal state for humanity and the natural world, and we will strive to design our futures to achieve this:

- **Humanity before technology** – we must consider our futures to be human-centric and meeting the overall needs of the communities within which people live. We must not select technologies purely on their merits – functional and offering a return on investment (ROI) – independent of those human needs. The success of the organization is just a reflection of the success of humanity and the natural systems we impact.
- **Plurality, inclusion and equity** – we must equally consider all members of the community, and the wider world, and provide them with ownership of our futures without exception. This extends to the built environment, technologies we utilize (and data we create), products we produce, the people we employ and the communities we serve.
- **Scientific fact, and creativity** – we embrace scientific progress and invention and apply our collective creativity to that in the context of the first two principles.

As a reflection, our dystopian principles provide the ability to imagine a trajectory that drives us to travel towards a state which will be suboptimal for humanity and the natural world, and we will imagine the struggles we will face by placing organizational goals first:

- **Technological solutions before humanity** – we consider our futures to be tech-centric. Therefore, we meet the goals of the organization to provide products and services that people must buy into to benefit – solution ideas ahead of human needs. The success of the organization is just a reflection of the success of the deployment of solutions and the profits generated by that.
- **Organizational growth and profit** – we must focus on exponential growth at any cost and use revenues and profits to represent success. While we celebrate and thank our customers / users, we ultimately include them in the technological solution stack as integral parts of the product, and not as individuals with basic needs.
- **Selective information, and creativity** – while we embrace scientific progress and invention, we choose smaller parts to embrace and reframe in the overall vision of the organization. We restrict our collective creativity to that in the context of the first two principles.

The ability to frame our inquiries, questioning and discussions using these is critical to the whole process.

Step 3: Setting Scanning Themes

Team Instructions: Outline scanning themes – i.e. areas of exploration – that inform the activities of signals scanning and identification of trends. This is an activity that would be completed ahead of any collaborative session and agreed upon by the organization and working group.

For our exercise we will explore the following scanning themes that will have effects on our futures:

- Food prices and logistics
- Global shifts on population and city growth
- Impacts of climate change
- Changing energy landscape

- Novel plant-based foods
- Cellular agriculture
- Pharma crops, plant-based medicines
- Urban and vertical farming
- Data growth, agritech, sensors and machine learning

Steps 4 and 5: Scan for signals and identify trends

Team Instructions: Using the guiding areas of exploration, look for signals using secondary research (academic articles, interviews, media articles, process-based and technical developments etc.) and then identify trends from them.

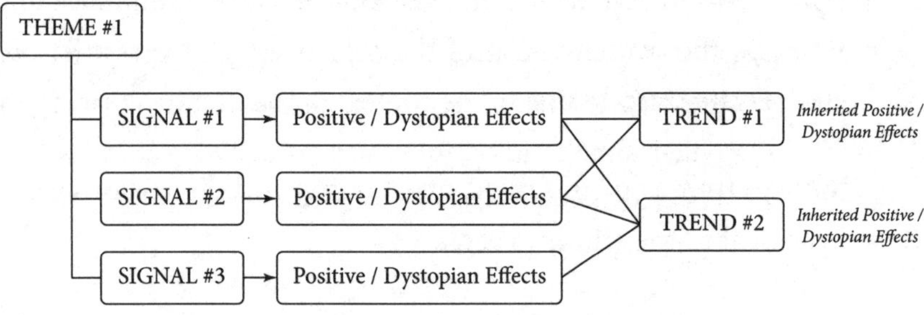

Fig 6.2 Signal to Positive / Dystopian effects to Trends

The numbering references we use are structured as S*<area of exploration number>.<signal number>* followed by the signal name e.g. 'S1.1 Food prices are rising globally' – this provides a useful way for tracking in the futures design and in subsequent work.

Note: We will see repeated positive and dystopian effects repeated on occasion. This can happen and indicates patterns in the signals analysis.

THEME (TH1): Food prices and logistics

- **S1.1 – Food prices are rising globally**

- Prices globally are up nearly 33 per cent since the same period in 2021, according to the UN Food and Agriculture Organization (FAO). From July, prices are up by over 3 per cent. Overall, this year the FAO's index puts food prices at levels not seen since 2011, the peak of rising prices spurred by weather shocks and high oil prices, which fuelled a global food price crisis and famously resulted in widespread protests ahead of the Arab Spring (source: *Fortune*[52]).
  - **Positive effects:**
    - The broken global supply chain can be studied.
    - The creation of more resilient local supply chains with foods based on seasons (in-field growing) and local food production in large cities through urban, rooftop and vertical farming.
  - **Dystopian effects:**
    - Nutritional food becomes unaffordable.
    - Food waste increases from 1.3 billion tons today (source: OzHarvest[53]).

- **S1.2 – Supply chain chaos is resulting in significant profits and delays**
  - Rates for Capesizes (bulkers with capacity of around 180,000 deadweight tons or DWT) surged 15 per cent on Monday to $52,900 per day, with rates for Panamaxes (65,000–90,000 DWT) and Supramaxes (45,000–60,000 DWT) at or near decade highs, at $32,400 and $34,900 per day, respectively. Even

[52] Katherine Dunn, 'First came the frost and drought. Now comes the rise in food prices', 2021, *Fortune*
[53] 'Food Waste Facts', 2022, OzHarvest

so, dry bulk rates are still nowhere near pinnacles reached in 2007–2008.

- Shares of Safe Bulkers jumped 17 per cent in five times the average trading volume on Monday. In general, shares of dry bulk stocks have risen by around 200–400 per cent over the past year, in several cases outpacing container stocks (source: Freightwaves[54]).
  - **Positive effects:**
    - There will be a new impetus for growing food locally and having a simplified supply chain.
  - **Dystopian effects:**
    - Food prices rise and set new ceilings for trade, knocking on into cost of living for the end consumers, which could lead to less access to nutritious food in both developed and developing nations.
    - The rise of food mega-corporations and their influence into global food dynamics.

IDENTIFIED TREND (TR1): Food prices and logistics costs are surging (post-pandemic)

THEME (TH2): Global Shifts on population and city growth

- **S2.1 – There will be a changing of the guard regarding economic superpowers (measured by GDP) by 2030, with China and India as #1 and #2 spots with the United States in at #3** (source: Statista[55])

[54] Shipping stocks hit fresh highs amid COVID-era supply chain chaos, 2021, *American Shipper*

[55] Aaron O'Neill, 'Gross domestic product (GDP) at current prices in China and the United States from 2005 to 2020 with forecasts until 2035', 2021, Statista

- In order – 1. China ($64.2 trillion); 2. India ($46.3 trillion); 3. United States ($31 trillion); 4. Indonesia ($10.1 trillion); 5. Turkey ($9.1 trillion); 6. Brazil ($8.6 trillion); 7. Egypt ($8.2 trillion); 8. Russia ($7.9 trillion); 9. Japan ($7.2 trillion); 10 Germany ($6.9 trillion).
    - **Positive effects**
        - Opening up of global trade for food commodities.
        - Sharing of IP internationally.
        - A new decade of collaboration.
    - **Dystopian effects**
        - China (1.4 billion people) and India (1.38 billion people) become the de facto ringleaders for decisions across Asia with influence extending into Africa (1.26 billion people).
        - Dalliances with mischief-makers like Russia regarding military and political support – especially with Russia-Ukraine tensions – leads to geopolitical struggles and even conflict regarding food access.

- **S2.2 – There will be explosive growth in the populations of Asia and even more so in Africa, especially in megacities, from 2022 to 2100**
    - The world's population might increase to 9.7 billion by 2050 and rise further to 11.2 billion by 2100. The expected global population growth is projected to be largely driven by increases in Asia and particularly in Africa. While the Asian population is expected to peak by 2050, Africa's population is projected to grow strongly and continuously, from 1.2 billion today to about 4.5 billion by 2100.
    - The total population of the EU-27 is projected to increase slightly from 505 million currently to 510 million by 2030, and

then to decrease in the subsequent decades to some 465 million by 2100 (source: European Environment Agency[56]).

- 2.5 billion people will shift to urban populations by 2050, 90 per cent of that will happen in Africa and Asia. Plus it is projected that India will have added 416 million urban dwellers, China 255 million and Nigeria 189 million (source: United Nations[57]).
- Megacities will be concentrated in Sub-Saharan Africa and Asia:

  1. Lagos, Nigeria (88,344,661 people); 2. Kinshasa, Democratic Republic of Congo (83,493,793); 3. Dar Es Salaam, United Republic of Tanzania (73,678,022) 4. Mumbai, India (67,239,804); 5. Delhi, India (57,334,134); 6. Khartoum, Sudan (56,594,472); 7. Niamey, Niger (56,149,130); 8. (Dhaka, Bangladesh (54,249,845); 9. Kolkata, India (52,395,315); 10. Kabul, Afghanistan (50,269,659) (source: Global Cities Institute[58]).

  - **Positive effects**
    - Growth of urban populations leads to growing economies and new opportunities for trade and the provision of food and medicine.
    - The creation of new models of business for megacities and communities growing their own food.
  - **Dystopian effects**
    - Reduced access to food.
    - The prevalence of food black markets and underground.

---

[56] 'Population trends 1950 – 2100: globally and within Europe', 2021, European Environment Agency

[57] 'Around 2.5 billion more people will be living in cities by 2050, projects new UN report', 2018, United Nations Department of Social Affairs

[58] Daniel Hoornweg and Kevin Pope, 'Socioeconomic Pathways and Regional Distribution of the World's 101 Largest Cities', 2014, Global Cities Institute

- The increased possibility of widespread foodborne illness.
- Increased need for healthcare.
- Increasing mortality rates due to malnutrition.

IDENTIFIED TREND (TR2): Population growth, and economic power is shifting

THEME (TH3): Impacts of climate change

- **S3.1 – a 40 per cent shortfall of available water across the globe by 2030 with effects not just for drinking, food production, hygiene and public health, but also for 98 per cent of global electric power generation** (source: Nature[59]), and a potential 35 per cent reduction in yields of global vegetable and legume production by 2100 due to water scarcity and increased salinity and ozone (source: PNAS[60]).
    - **Positive effects**
        - An urgency will be created for water-efficient growing systems (potentially indoor farming like vertical farming).
        - New in-field techniques and solutions will be created.
    - **Dystopian effects**
        - The loss of water-intensive crops and farming practices – growing almonds and raising cattle potentially.

IDENTIFIED TREND (TR3): Global climate impacts on water usage for electric generation and food production

---

[59] 'Global power generation could be severely affected by predicted 40% global water shortfall in 2030', 2016, Nature, World Energy Council

[60] Pauline F. D. Scheelbeek, 'Effect of environmental changes on vegetable and legume yields and nutritional quality', 2018, PNAS

THEME (TH4): Changing energy landscape

- **S4.1 – 100 per cent Clean and Renewable Wind, Water and Sunlight All-Sector Energy Roadmaps for 139 Countries of the World have been developed (theorized) to reduce reliance on fossil fuels.** 'We develop roadmaps to transform the all-purpose energy infrastructures (electricity, transportation, heating / cooling, industry, agriculture / forestry / fishing) of 139 countries to ones powered by wind, water, and sunlight (WWS)' (source: Stanford[61]).
    - **Positive effects**
        - **Simplification of energy generation will deliver cost benefits** – The roadmaps envision 80 per cent conversion by 2030 and 100 per cent by 2050. WWS not only replaces business-as-usual (BAU) power, but also reduces it 42.5 per cent because the work–energy ratio of WWS electricity exceeds that of combustion (23.0 per cent); WWS requires no mining, transporting, or processing of fuels (12.6 per cent); and WWS end-use efficiency is assumed to exceed that of BAU (6.9 per cent).
        - **The workforce will shift and create new jobs** – Converting to WWS may create 24.3 million more permanent, full-time jobs than jobs lost.
        - **Reduces pollution-related deaths** – It may avoid 4.6 million/year premature air-pollution deaths today and 3.5 million/year in 2050.

[61] Mark Z. Jacobson, Mark A. Delucchi, Zack A.F. Bauer, Jingfan Wang, Eric Weiner, Alexander S. Yachanin, '100% Clean and Renewable Wind, Water, and Sunlight All-Sector Energy Roadmaps for 139 Countries of the World', Joule / Stanford

        - **Reduced pollution and climate costs** – $22.8 trillion/year in 2050 air-pollution costs; and $28.5 trillion/year in 2050 climate costs. Transitioning should also stabilize energy prices because fuel costs are significantly lower, reduce power disruption and increase access to energy by decentralizing power, and avoid 1.5°C global warming.
    - **Dystopian effects**
        - **Energy wars** – fuelled by discontent in the large energy providers we see today and increased lobbying, the spreading of misinformation and the disruption of renewable energy companies and initiatives.

- **S4.2 – new independent farm-level energy production is possible, both to provide energy for farming operations and to sell back into the grid.**
    - **Agrovoltaics – placing solar arrays above crops – could present opportunities to farmers, as could technologies such as anaerobic digesters that use food waste to create methane that burns and creates electricity.**
        - **Positive effects**
            - Increased revenues for farmers and energy independence to support the electrification of operations.
            - Land usage opportunities – 'Hypothetically, if all the lettuce grown in the U.S. were converted to agrovoltaic systems, it could double the nation's entire installed photovoltaic capacity' (source: Dinesh and Pearce[62]).

[62] Harshavardhan Dinesh and Joshua M. Pearce, 'The potential of agrivoltaic systems', 2016, Renewable and Sustainable Energy Reviews

        - Reduces methane emissions and finds a use for food waste from farming operations to local supermarkets and the food supply chain.
    - **Dystopian effects**
        - Good, arable farmland is acquired and converted to agrovoltaics, thus reducing the amount of food grown.
        - CO_2 is still released by burning methane.

- **S4.3 – Global super grids will revolutionize energy and the effort will be spearheaded by China and Asian and European countries** – China's own technocratic vision for a global supergrid envisages high-voltage interconnection crossing continents and the ocean. By 2050 it promises 720 gigawatts of transboundary power flow, at an estimated cost of US$38 trillion, including US$11 trillion in power grid investment (source: China Dialogue[63]). And there is the possibility of a European supergrid – a possible future supergrid – that would ultimately interconnect the various European countries and the regions around Europe's borders – including North Africa, Kazakhstan and Turkey – with a high-voltage direct current (HVDC) power grid (source: Claverton Energy Research Group[64]).
    - **Positive effects**
        - The changing of the energy production and distribution business model with falling energy prices and real-time, cross-border trading.
    - **Dystopian effects**
        - Energy increasingly becomes a geopolitical tool, enabling cuts to the supply of energy, water and food and / or trade

[63] Eugene Simonov, 'The risks of a global supergrid', 2018, China Dialogue
[64] Dave Andrews, 'Why Do We Need The Supergrid, What Is Its Scope And What Will It Achieve?', 2019, Claverton Energy Research Group

disputes e.g. China and Russia come together to annex North America's access to this super grid supply via cables under the Baring Sea. Something we are starting to see play out with the Russia-Ukraine conflict.

IDENTIFIED TREND (TR4): The increase in energy-generating (energy independent) farms and electrification

THEME (TH5): Novel plant-based foods

- **S5.1 – 2018 Global vegan food market was valued at $14.2 billion in 2018, and is expected to reach $31.4 billion by 2026, registering a CAGR of 10.5 per cent from 2019 to 2026** (source: Allied Market Research[65]).
    - **Positive effects**
        - Less reliance on industrialized beef, pork, chicken farming and the risks associated with that – methane pollution, water usage (including feed growth).
    - **Dystopian effects**
        - Radicalization of both meat eaters and vegetarians / vegans and misinformation campaigns leading to protests.
- **S5.2 – COVID is accelerating demand for plant-based options.** Gallup survey found that 77 per cent of Americans had reduced their meat consumption in past twelve months (source: Gallup[66]).
    - **Positive effects**

[65] 'Vegan Food Market by Product Type (Dairy Alternative, Meat Substitute and others) and Distribution Channel (Offline and Online): Global Opportunity Analysis and Industry Forecast 2021–2030', 2022, Allied Market Research

[66] Marc Coloma, '2021 Will Be The Year That Plant-Based Foods Will Finally Go Mainstream', 2021, *Food & Beverage Magazine*

        - Less reliance on industrialized beef, pork, chicken farming and the risks associated with that – methane pollution, water usage (including feed growth).
        - New plant-based food developed.
        - Healthier plant-based diets.
    - **Dystopian effects**
        - The industrialized beef, pork, chicken farming industry strikes and causes political upheaval, supported by fast food producers and restaurants.

- **S5.3 – Consumers are starting to choose plant-based**
    - 2020 – International sandwich shop Pret A Manager ($2B valuation) expands vegetarian-only stores that cater to 'ecotarians' (Plant Based News[67]); large US grocer, Kroger, moves plant-based meat products into meat aisle, improving sales on average 23 per cent (source: IGD[68], PBFA[69]).
    - 2021 – Berlin's university canteens go almost meat-free as students prioritize climate[70]; UK Premier League football stadium – Tottenham Hotspur Stadium – plan to be the world's first net zero carbon fixture, including food kiosks offering plant-based food options (source: BBC[71]); Nestlé; Professional Cool Food Meals will incorporate plant-based proteins from

---

[67] Maria Chiorando, 'Pret A Manger To Open 7 New Veggie Pret Stores This Summer', 2020, Plant Based News

[68] Hannah Skeggs, 'Segregation or integration – Ranging plant-based products to drive sales', 2021, IGD

[69] 'PBFA and Kroger Plant-Based Meat Study', 2020, Plant Based Foods Association

[70] Philip Oltermann, 'Berlin's university canteens go almost meat-free as students prioritise climate', 2021, *Guardian*

[71] 'Tottenham v Chelsea: Premier League tie to be first net zero carbon football match', 2021, *BBC Sport*

Sweet Earth Foods, which will be carbon neutral by 2025 (source: Sustainable Brands[72]).

- **Positive effects**
  - The plant-based industry attracts increased funding to accelerate growth.
  - Cultural change towards plant-based foods.
- **Dystopian effects**
  - A pro-meat grassroots revolution could be established and there would be vandalism, violence and arson relating to plant-based retail food outlets.

- **S5.4 – 'Sales of plant-based dairy and meat alternatives reached US$29.4 billion in 2020, and could increase to US$162 billion by 2030, comprising 7.7 per cent of the global protein market. Alternative dairy alone could double by 2030 buoyed by the popularity of oat milk and growth in ice cream, cheese and butter alternatives'** (source: BNN Bloomberg[73]).
  - **Positive effects**
    - Less reliance on the meat and dairy industrial complex.
  - **Dystopian effects**
    - A pro-meat grassroots revolution could be established and there would be vandalism, violence and arson relating to plant-based retail food outlets.

IDENTIFIED TREND (TR5): Plant-based (and sustainable) nutrition is becoming mainstream

---

[72] 'Nestlé Professional, WRI Expand Cool Food Meals to Foodservice Locations Across the US', 2021, Sustainable Brands

[73] Elizabeth Elkin, 'Plant-based food sales to increase fivefold by 2030', 2021, *Bloomberg News*

THEME (TH6): Cellular agriculture

- **S6.1** – 73 per cent increase in demand for protein by 2050, and the meat market will be worth $7.3 trillion (WIRED[74]).
- **S6.2** – New sustainable proteins (plant, meat, seafood, dairy), created by cellular agriculture, are racing onto the markets. They are touted to be more affordable to feed a growing global population and reduce the world carbon footprint as 25 per cent of CO_2 emissions currently due to food production (source: Gallup[75]).
    - **Positive effects**
        - The cellular agriculture industry starts to eat into the market share of protein consumed, with a reduction both of the water needed and pollution.
    - **Dystopian effects**
        - The cost of 'real protein' will skyrocket, making it less affordable to purchase and leading to a protein deficit in less affluent demographics.

- **S6.3** – 'By 2030, demand for cow products will have fallen by 70 per cent. Before we reach this point, the U.S. cattle industry will be effectively bankrupt. By 2035, demand for cow products will have shrunk by 80–90 per cent. Other livestock markets such as chicken, pig, and fish will follow a similar trajectory' (source: RethinkX[76]).
    - **Positive effects**

---

[74] Matt Simon, 'Lab-Grown Meat Is Coming, Whether You Like It or Not', 2018, WIRED

[75] Marc Coloma, '2021 Will Be The Year That Plant-Based Foods Will Finally Go Mainstream', 2021, *Food & Beverage Magazine*

[76] Catherine Tubb and Tony Seba, 'Rethinking Food and Agriculture 2020-2030', 2019, RethinkX

        - Protein can be grown without extensive land and water usage, and wherever we want – even at a local scale. The at-restaurant or at-home of protein will allow for starter cells to be shipped to locations where they are used to grow protein, much like Coca-Cola ships syrup to quick service restaurants.
        - The protein bioreactor market will grow rapidly.
    - **Dystopian effects**
        - Mass-unemployment in the raised protein industry.
        - Million-dollar thoroughbred pigs, chickens, cows raised, causing bidding wars for the best quality 'starter cells' thus driving up the cost of cellular protein.

IDENTIFIED TREND (TR6): The raised protein industry will be significantly disrupted by cellular protein production

THEME (TH7): Pharma crops, plant-based medicines

- **S7.1 – A number of crops can be grown with applications in the pharmaceutical world** – for example, vegetable oils (vitamin E); beetroot (geosmin, used in perfumes); various herbs, including thyme (caffeic acid, used in cancer, immune system and anti-inflammatory treatments), valerian (valerenic acids, used for sleeping disorders) and astralagus root (astragenol, used for cardiac conditions); spices, including ginger (gingerol, used in arthritis and cancer treatment) and guinea pepper (paradol, an antioxidant); tobacco (deoxystreptamine, used in antibiotics); (source Verticalfarming.com[77]).
    - **Positive effects**

[77] 'Part 2: Pharmaceutical Crops', 2022, Vertical Farming

        - Diversity in crop production.
        - Decentralized growing of crops needed in the pharmaceutical industry.
    - **Dystopian effects**
        - The effects of climate change are felt in the Big Pharma industry as well.
        - Crop theft.

IDENTIFIED TREND (TR7): Farmers will diversify their crops and collaborate with Big Pharma for ingredients for pharmaceuticals

THEME (TH8): Pharma crops / plant-based medicines

- **S8.1 – Stress and trauma is endemic in society** – A study on the 'Future of Life in America'[78] found that younger Americans were reporting significantly higher rates of life stress. Among those aged 16 to 29, almost half (48 per cent) reported experiencing financial stress most or every day, 43 per cent reported experiencing family stress most or every day, and 35 per cent reported experiencing work stress most or every day. Younger Americans were also more likely to report significantly higher rates of loneliness and insecurity, with 47 per cent often feeling isolated from other people, 47 per cent often feeling left out by other people, 50 per cent often worried that other people were judging them, and 40 per cent often worried that other people might hurt them.
- **S8.2 – Plants can affect the brains and mental states of the humans who ingest them** – HC and CBD from cannabis; Psilocybin from

[78] 'The future of life in America: 2020 report', 2020, Intensions Consulting and Nikolas Badminton

'magic' mushrooms; Ayahuasca / DMT; Ibogaine from the Iboga root; Peyote; Salvia (source: Britannica[79]).

- **S8.3 – Psychedelic drugs market size is projected to reach $10.75 billion by 2027** – Data Bridge Market Research analyzes that the market is growing with a CAGR of 16.3 per cent in the forecast period of 2020 to 2027 and expected to reach USD $6,859.95 million by 2027 from USD 2,077.90 million in 2019. Growing acceptance of psychedelic drugs for treating depression and increasing prevalence of depression and mental disorders are the factors for the market growth (source: Data Bridge Market Research[80]).
    - **Positive effects**
        - The reliance on Big Pharma to provide drugs will be diminished and replaced with plant-based medicines like DMT, psilocybin and ibogaine.
        - Indigenous knowledge of plant-based medicines will be celebrated.
        - The healing of multigenerational trauma through combined usage alongside guided journeying and therapy.
    - **Dystopian effects**
        - Increased misuse of over-the-counter psychedelic compounds.
        - Misinformation campaigns by Big Pharma and bad actors (troll farms, state-sponsored actors).
        - The abuse of indigenous knowledge and adaption of usage to occur outside of ceremony.

[79] Melissa Petruzzello, '9 Mind-Altering Plants', Britannica

[80] 'Psychedelic Drugs Market Size Is Projected To Reach $10.75 Billion By 2027', 2021, Financial News media, Data Bridge Market Research

IDENTIFIED TREND (TR8): The plant-based medicine industry will grow significantly in concert with the increased need for therapies and mental health treatments

THEME (TH9): Urban and vertical farming

- **S9.1** – 'Vertical farming allows 100x more produce per square metre, 250 times less water than traditional farming and zero food miles since food is grown locally. Indoors with no soil, no pesticides, no contamination, less waste and can be located anywhere: near populations, near inexpensive renewable electricity' (source: *NY Times*[81], Agritecture[82]).
- **S9.2** – The global vertical farming market is projected to grow at a CAGR of 25.2 per cent from 2021 to 2028 – from USD$3.64 billion in 2021 to USD$17.59 billion in 2028 (source: Fortune Business Insights[83]).
- **S9.3** – 'In 2020, $929 million poured into U.S. indoor-farming ventures, more than double the investments in 2019. Mainly due to decreasing arable land, increasing market demand for local, sustainable produce, and migration towards mega-cities' (source: Crain's[84], Future Farming[85]).
- **S9.4 – Vertical farming businesses are gaining in value and delivering food at-scale:** In the year 2021: The company Unfold, established by Bayer AG & Singapore sovereign fund Temasek,

---

[81] 'No Soil. No Growing Seasons. Just Add Water and Technology', 2021, *The New York Times*

[82] 'The largest vertical farm in the world in one of the smallest countries', 2021, *Agritecture*

[83] 'Vertical Farming Market Size, Share & COVID-19 Impact Analysis…', 2021, Fortune Business Insights

[84] Ryan Deffenbaugh, 'The city's high-tech vertical farmers have been boosted by pandemic demand', 2020, Crain's New York Business

[85] 'Vertical farming needs to expand with fruiting crops', 2021, Future Farming

targeting vertical farms to utilize seed genetics rights initially for vegetables (lettuce, spinach, tomato, pepper, cucumber). Helping Singapore meet its goal of 30 per cent of food sourced domestically by 2030 (source: AG Funder News[86]); and, Bowery Farming, largest vertical farm in the US is now valued at $2.3 billion (source: Bloomberg[87]).

- **Positive effects**
  - More food can be grown closer to, or within, large cities with reduced land acreage, water and the need for fertilizers and weed killers.
  - Greens, vegetables and fruit can be grown more quickly and at lower cost once scale and energy independence (through solar) is achieved.
- **Dystopian effects**
  - Food costs can be set at premium levels due to accessibility and nutritional content, thus not serving populations that struggle with affording good quality food.

- **S9.5 – Urban farms have the potential to provide around 10 per cent of global vegetable crops, which could translate into big savings for local economies worldwide.** Start-up costs, however, are still high. Those involved in urban farming typically work longer than average hours, lose more food than rural farmers due to urban pests, and struggle to find skilled and experienced staff (source: Bloomberg CityLab[88]).

[86] Jack Ellis, 'Bayer & Temasek launch $30m seed genetics business targeting vertical farms', 2020, *AFN*

[87] Josyana Joshua, 'Farm Startup With Ties to NYC History Hits $2.3 Billion in Value', 2021, Bloomberg

[88] Amy Crawford, 'Big Data Suggests Big Potential for Urban Farming', 2018, Bloomberg CityLab

- **Positive effects**
    - Big savings for local economies worldwide.
    - Improving food security and reducing poverty among the poorest by providing cheaper and more easily available food.
    - Health benefits of providing affordable nutritious fruit, vegetables and organically produced meat.
    - Greater social inclusion by providing local job opportunities and, in the case of community projects, bringing communities together.
    - Educational opportunities for children, e.g. school trips to city farms and community gardens, where pupils can learn more about where food comes from.
- **Dystopian effects**
    - Start-up costs are high. Those involved in urban farming typically work longer than average hours, lose more food than rural farmers due to urban pests, and struggle to find skilled and experienced staff.
    - Food costs can be set at premium levels due to accessibility and nutritional content, thus not serving populations that struggle with affording good quality food.

IDENTIFIED TREND (TR9): Indoor and vertical farming is starting to grow exponentially

THEME (TH10): Data growth, agritech, sensors and machine learning

- **S10.1 – The total amount of data created, captured, copied and consumed globally is forecast to increase rapidly**, reaching 64.2 zettabytes in 2020. And, over the next five years up to 2025, global data creation is projected to grow to more than 180 zettabytes with a (CAGR) of 23 per cent over the period 2020–2025 (source: IDC[89]).

- **Positive effects**
    - Access to more granular data leads to a greater ability to divine insights that drive better strategic planning.
- **Dystopian effects**
    - An overwhelming effort is created to capture and process all data that leads to larger costs vs ROI.
    - No consideration of data biases influencing strategy.

- **S10.2 – 'Advances in artificial intelligence (AI) will have massive social consequences.** Self-driving technology could potentially replace millions of driving jobs over the coming decade. In addition to possible unemployment, the transition will bring new challenges, such as rebuilding infrastructure, protecting vehicle cyber-security, and adapting laws and regulations.'(source: 'When Will AI Exceed Human Performance? Evidence from AI Experts' (Grace et al)[90]).
- **S10.3 – 'Researchers predict AI will outperform humans in many activities in the next 10 years**, such as translating languages (by 2024), writing high-school essays (by 2026), driving a truck (by 2027), working in retail (by 2031), writing a bestselling book (by 2049), and working as a surgeon (by 2053). Researchers believe there is a 50 per cent chance of AI outperforming humans in all tasks in 45 years and of automating all human jobs in 120 years, with Asian respondents expecting these dates much sooner that North

[89] 'Data Creation and Replication Will Grow at a Faster Rate than Installed Storage Capacity, According to the IDC Global DataSphere and StorageSphere Forecasts', 2021, IDC

[90] Katja Grace, John Salvatier, Allan Dafoe, Baobao Zhang, and Owain Evans, 'When Will AI Exceed Human Performance? Evidence from AI Experts', 2018, *Journal of Artificial Intelligence Research*

Americans' (source: 'When Will AI Exceed Human Performance? Evidence from AI Experts' (Grace et al)[91]).

- **S10.4 – $15.7 trillion could be added to the global economy by 2030 due to increased productivity and consumption side-effects** (of machine learning / artificial intelligence systems) (source: PwC[92]).
    - **Positive effects**
        - More productive humans with simple tasks taken over by collaborative robots ('cobots') and AI system work.
        - Greater accuracy.
        - Faster completion of tasks and greater throughput of work.
        - The ability to free humans from 'algorithmic work' where a low level of cognitive skill is needed, e.g. quick service restaurant cook or teller, taxi driver etc.
        - 100 per cent autonomous operations with human oversight.
    - **Dystopian effects**
        - Policy decisions made in support of pureplay automation (independent robot and system work).
        - 100 per cent autonomous operations with no oversight and an inability to make 'human' ethical and empathetic judgements.
        - Increased cybersecurity threats.

- **S10.5 – In-field communications will gain resiliency through satellite and mesh communications:** Starlink is aiming for < 20 milliseconds target latency and immediate benefit for rural, remote

[91] Katja Grace, John Salvatier, Allan Dafoe, Baobao Zhang, and Owain Evans, 'When Will AI Exceed Human Performance? Evidence from AI Experts', 2018, *Journal of Artificial Intelligence Research*

[92] PwC, 'Sizing the prize', 2022, pwc.com

and unconnected locations with 4,400 low-Earth orbit Starlink satellites deployed by 2024, and 12,000 low-Earth orbit Starlink satellites in-orbit by 2027; Mesh Networks are growing to be an $8 billion market by 2026. This will deliver high network coverage and scalable deployment without the requirement of cabling each access pointer/router, and resilient and cheaper to set up – reduced installation costs and deployment complexities (source: GlobalNewsWire[93]).

- **Positive effects**
  - More resilient communications.
  - The ability to deploy more technological systems over wider areas previously not within mobile service areas.
- **Dystopian effects**
  - Costs of rural location communications will be controlled by very few providers.
  - Communications infrastructures become centralized and targets for independent and state-sponsored hackers.

- **S10.6 – The installed base of active internet of things connected devices is forecast to reach 30.9 billion units by 2025** (source: Statista[94]).
- **S10.7 – The global internet of things market size is projected to reach USD$1.46 trillion by 2027 while exhibiting a CAGR of 24.9 per cent from 2021 to 2027** (source: Fortune Business Insights[95]).

[93] 'Wireless Mesh Network Market revenue to hit USD 8 Bn by 2026, growing at around 15%', 2020, *Global Market Insights*

[94] Lionel Sujay Vailshery, 'Internet of Things (IoT) – statistics & facts', 2022, *Statista*

[95] 'Internet of Things (IoT) Market Worth USD 1463.19 Billion by 2027 Backed by Rising Awareness Regarding Precision Farming to Aid Market Growth', 2021, Fortune Business Insights

- **S10.8 – The IoT in agriculture market size was valued at $ 16,330 million in 2017, and is projected to reach $48,714 million by 2025, growing at a CAGR of 14.7 per cent from 2018 to 2025** (source: Allied Market Research[96]).
    - **Positive effects**
        - Remote monitoring of livestock and crops.
        - Real-time data capture and transmission.
        - Precision farming capabilities are made possible – and consider scientific measurement, observation and analytics to draw conclusions and inform corrective actions.
    - **Dystopian effects**
        - Increasingly complex agricultural systems architected to include sensors and automation create increased investments and maintenance.
        - Increased exposure to cybersecurity threats.

- **S10.9 – In 2021 just over $4.3 billion was invested in the agritech sector across 263 deals.** (source: Crop Life[97]).
- **S10.10** – The following areas are where investments are made: value chain & logistics, food / feed / fuel ingredients, crop protection/ production, digital agriculture, animal health/nutrition (source: Crop Life[98]).
    - **Positive effects**
        - The ability to have access to new technologies to help with Value Chain & Logistics, Food / Feed / Fuel Ingredients,

[96] 'IOT in Agriculture Market…', 2018, *Allied Market Research*

[97] Kyle Welborn, '2021 Mid-Year AgTech Venture Capital Investment Round Up', 2021, *CropLife*

[98] Kyle Welborn, '2021 Mid-Year AgTech Venture Capital Investment Round Up', 2021, *CropLife*

Crop Protection/Production, Digital Agriculture, Animal Health/Nutrition will lead to more resilient food systems.

- **Dystopian effects**
  - Significantly sized food producers will have access to these technologies ahead of smaller operations, thus creating more pressure regarding the price of food and ability to scale.
  - The price of food will be increased to offset the investment needed to build out

IDENTIFIED TREND (TR10): Data growth, agritech, sensors and machine learning

Steps 6 and 7: Write Positive and Dystopian Scenarios (speculative solutions, impacts, and risks)

Team Instructions: There are two parts to this, and this is about the distillation of ideas to create more succinct scenarios:

***Part One** – take three of the trends that show the most promise, take the signals that feed into them, and identify opportunities and challenges from the positive and dystopian effects that have been identified. Then create a list of 3 to 5 speculative solutions that could exist to serve these trends. This provides a comprehensive view at this point, which can be discussed prior to reducing to succinct scenarios in the next two steps.*

***Part Two** – take three solutions, identify the business opportunities and risks, and then explore impacts across Organizational, Cultural, Environmental, and Technological development. Then structure them into a WHAT IF... scenario, as follows:*

What if in the [2040s]
solutions
[a, b, and c are implemented],
which creates these
[opportunities and risks],
and impacts
[Organizational, Cultural, Environmental, and Technological development].

From this we are able to imagine what 3 to 5 speculative solutions could be to serve these trends. This provides a comprehensive view at this point that can be discussed prior to reducing it into succinct scenarios in part two. For example:

SCENARIO 1: An agricultural future driven by renewable energy infrastructure, vertical farming and cellular protein production.

TREND 4: The increase in energy-generating (energy independent) farms and electrification

- **Positive effects** (creating opportunities)
    - Simplification of energy generation will deliver cost benefits.
    - The workforce will shift and create new jobs.
    - Reduces pollution-related deaths, and reduced pollution and climate costs.
    - Increased revenues for farmers and energy independence to support the electrification of operations.
    - Land usage opportunities.
    - Reduce methane emissions and finds a use for food waste.

- **Dystopian effects** (identifying risks)
  - Energy wars between grid energy providers and farmers.
  - Good, arable farmland is acquired and converted to agrovoltaics, thus reducing the amount of food grown.
  - CO_2 is still released by burning methane although it is a lot better than fossil fuels.
  - The changing of the energy production and distribution business model with falling energy prices and real-time, cross-border trading.
  - Energy increasingly becomes a geopolitical tool.

- **Speculative solutions that can be developed** (creating business value)
  - **Energy provision agreements** – between grid energy providers and farmers to ensure harmony across energy generation and transmission
  - **New innovations in on-farm energy production** – that doesn't greatly affect crop yields – agrovoltaics, anaerobic digestion
  - **The creation of independent farm-to-farm / farm-to-community microgrids** – providing cheap power and new revenue streams

TREND 6: The raised protein industry will be significantly disrupted by cellular protein production

- ***Positive effects*** *(creating opportunities)*
  - The cellular agriculture industry starts to eat into the market share of protein consumed, reducing both the water needed and pollution.
  - Protein can be grown without extensive land, water usage and wherever we want – even at a local scale. The 'Coca-

Cola-ization' of protein where starter cells are shipped to locations, where they are used to grow protein, much like Coca-Cola ships syrup to quick service restaurants.
  - The industrial-scale protein bioreactor market will grow rapidly.

- ***Dystopian effects*** *(identifying risks)*
  - The cost of 'real protein' will skyrocket – making it less affordable to purchase and leading to a protein deficit in less affluent demographics.
  - Mass-unemployment in the raised protein industry.
  - Million-dollar thoroughbred pigs, chickens, cows raised causing bidding wars for the best quality 'starter cells', thus driving up the cost of cellular protein.
  - The disruption of cultural traditions – Thanksgiving (turkeys) and religious holidays etc.

- ***Speculative solutions that can be developed*** *(creating business value)*
  - ***Global market for starter cells*** *– pork, chicken, beef, seafood.*
  - ***Thoroughbred animal farms*** *– for premium starter farms and the preservation of mainstream and heritage breeds.*
  - ***Commissary-scale protein production*** *– to serve dark / ghost kitchens.*
  - ***Community-scale bioreactor facilities*** *– built into trucks to allow movement around the state to areas where protein is most needed (and for provision to military and emergency response operations).*
  - ***Repurposing of farms where animals were raised to energy production areas*** *– wind, solar and geothermal.*

TREND 9: Indoor and vertical farming is starting to grow exponentially

- ***Positive effects*** *(creating opportunities)*
    - More food can be grown closer to, or within, large cities with reduced land acreage, water and the need for fertilizers and weed killers.
    - Greens, vegetables and fruit can be grown more quickly and at lower cost once scale and energy independence (through solar) is achieved.
    - Big savings for local economies worldwide.
    - Improving food security and reducing poverty by providing cheaper and more easily available food.
    - Health benefits of providing affordable nutritious fruit, vegetables and organically produced meat.
    - Greater social inclusion by providing local job opportunities and, in the case of community projects, bringing communities together.
    - Educational opportunities for children, e.g. school trips to city farms and community gardens where pupils can learn more about where food comes from.

- **Dystopian effects** (identifying risks)
    - Food costs can be set at premium levels due to accessibility and nutritional content, thus not serving populations that struggle to afford good quality food.
    - Start-up costs are high. Those involved in urban farming typically work longer than average hours, lose more food than rural farmers due to urban pests, and struggle to find skilled and experienced staff.

- **Speculative solutions that can be developed** (creating business value)
  - ***Community vertical and urban farms*** *– can be developed together on limited land and rooftops to provide affordable food.*
  - ***Industrial-scale vertical farms*** *– provide greens to the foodservice industry across cities, reducing pressure on in-field farming.*

In Part Two of the Positive-Dystopian framework we further distil the thinking by taking three solutions, identifying the business opportunities and risks, and then exploring impacts across Organizational, Cultural, Environmental and Technological development. Then structure them into a WHAT IF… scenario, as follows:

What if in the *[2040s]*
[community-focused farm-to-community microgrids, cellular protein production and vertical / urban farms are implemented],
which creates these

(Business) Opportunities

- Increased revenues for farmers and energy independence to support the electrification of operations.
- Land usage opportunities – shifting from reliance on food production.
- Industrial-scale protein bioreactor developments.
- Protein can be grown without extensive land and water usage, and wherever we want.
- City-based, at-scale food production facilities.
- Improved food security and reducing poverty among the poorest by providing cheaper and more easily available food.

- Greater social inclusion by providing local job opportunities and, in the case of community projects, bringing communities together.

...and

(Business and Societal) Risks

- Energy wars between grid energy providers and farmers, and energy increasingly becomes a geopolitical tool.
- Good, arable farmland is acquired and converted to agrovoltaics, thus reducing the amount of food grown and eventually becoming the dominant revenue generator thus leading to the abandonment of food production.
- The cost of 'real protein' will skyrocket – making it less affordable to purchase and causing tensions in countries where consuming meat is culturally significant.
- Food costs (for urban-produced protein, greens and vegetables) are manipulated to facilitate 'growth and adoption', thus having a knock-on effect on other parts of the food supply chain, and those farmers (potentially putting many multigenerational farms out of business).
- Start-up costs are high. Those involved in urban farming typically work longer than average hours, lose more food than rural farmers due to urban pests, and struggle to find skilled and experienced staff.

and impacts

Organizational factors

- The structuring of companies to ensure that food and energy is affordable and that the community has ownership of the solutions, and an ability to advise, provided in addition to Organization X driving growth and profit.

- The interplay of People (hierarchy, skills, relationships), Process (how the human and technological systems hold together), and Governance (the accountability and rules within the organization) needs to be understood.
- New rules and regulations and the lobbying of the government for positive change and awareness of risks (identified above).

Cultural factors

- Tradition and ritual are upended and a new age of tradition will need to be established, i.e. growing synth-turkey using starter cells in a bioreactor for Thanksgiving.
- Family togetherness centred around food needs to be considered.

Environmental factors

- Reduced water usage while generating more food and energy.
- New environmental factors – facility production, waste etc. needs to be managed transparently.

Technological factors

- Complex technological farming systems require new capabilities in existing farms – data scientists, machine learning experts, cybersecurity experts, platform and machinery experts

Steps 6 and 7 (an additional activity): Look ahead and back at our horizons

Team Instructions: Now that we have baseline scenarios in place, we have the ability to look ahead at both the 2050s to see how this may progress over time, and back to the 2030s to understand what we may have to aim for in the interim to create our scenarios.

We can take a higher-level view of what we may expect to experience and see in these horizons.

2050s – a world with food sovereignty

- Holistic and sustainable water-food-energy systems that serve the largest and most exposed cities in the world.
- Community empowerment and relationships that change the shape of these systems to ensure adaptability in the face of new challenges.

2040s – a new world of urban food production

- New capabilities are bedding in.
- Cultural change and acceptance is underway for vertical farming and cellular agriculture.
- New brands, products, rituals and traditions are established and gain pace.
- New business models around community empowerment in modern business are adopted.

2030s – a world in transition

- Investments and partnerships.
- Government relations and initiatives.
- Disruption of existing industries of food production and energy.
- Cultural change and getting the public on board with the vision we can develop for our equitable world.

Taking time to reflect

When we have worked through things together, this should all feel possible with empowerment of communities and a balance that creates a more equitable world. It's inevitable that some legacy businesses and individuals unwilling to adapt will start the journey to becoming obsolete or falling victim to market and competitive forces, experiencing the potentiality of collapse in a real and visceral way.

Steps 1 to 7 of the Positive-Dystopian Framework will provide a huge amount of reference material and through its reductive method lead us to scenarios that show us succinct views of our futures.

I recommend that organizations should stop and reflect on the work at this point. It is also important to share this work internally with all employees. The beauty of futures work is to inspire ideas of what we may become. Gaining a broad perspective, even from those that have not been a part of the futures design activity undertaken, is essential.

Organizations should create the ability for additional ideas to be shared, upvoted and built upon. It can also be advantageous in sharing these ideas – once agreed upon – with strategic partners as well.

Note: I do *not* recommend sharing with customers and the public at this stage unless there has been a strategic public consultation offered as part of a wider programme. I have seen this work well; the key is to carefully present the ideas as speculative and to gain external perspective in the frame of this speculative work.

Step 8: Speculative Fiction and Experiential Futures

Team Instructions: Take the full set of scenarios and all of the information and look further than the 2050 time frame into a world far from reality today. Sculpt stories, create marketing materials, make videos (animation and real action), write short and long form fiction, and make these visions of our futures come to life through storytelling.

In Chapter 7: Igniting Imagination we will deep dive into the process of Speculative Fiction and Experiential Futures and highlight incredible examples of storytelling from some of our world's most incredible futures explorers.

Broadening our perspectives

As I was writing this example, it became abundantly clear that it had a North American focus. I got into this with one of my great friends, Rafeeq Bosch – a Strategic Foresight Consultant and candidate for PhD in Futures Studies at Stellenbosch University in South Africa. He asked:

> 'Would it be very disruptive to our narrative stream to relocate the example away from the US to encourage a more global sensibility? China is much more interesting nowadays, or what about the next unicorn to rise in South America? I always flinch when I think about the US in the future, because more and more I believe the US is the UK of the twenty-first century. As America's economic and cultural movements and influence wanes, its last bastion will probably be its military (technological) dominance. But my point is not about picking winners and losers, but more just to shift the conversation away from incumbents.'

Bosch makes a great point and it's clear that the shifting economic power dynamics, population growth and shift to urban centres will take place in Africa, India and China. In fact, China will be the number one economic power (by GDP) by 2030 or sooner,[99] with India at number two, and the United States in third position. The UN Department of Economic and Social Affairs (DESA) are predicting that, 'together, India, China and Nigeria will account for 35 per cent

[99] Naomi Xu Elegant, 'China's 2020 GDP means it will overtake U.S. as world's No. 1 economy sooner than expected', 2021, Fortune

of the projected growth of the world's urban population between 2018 and 2050…It is projected that India will have added 416 million urban dwellers, China 255 million and Nigeria 189 million.'[100]

We should not consider these signals lightly; undertake some secondary research and suddenly assume we understand these places and the dynamics within them. In my research I regularly reach out to people in the places I reference to gain additional perspectives and insights, though this would fall short in a more in-depth futures design project.

To do that, there are a number of recommended practices to consider when pushing our thinking in other jurisdictions, and these also count for undertaking any futures design project using the Positive-Dystopian Framework:

- **Seek local knowledge** – The client team working on futures design must include most of its contributors from the countries / continents we are considering, or a mix of contributors if we choose to look at several jurisdictions. Over and above that, it is prudent to go further and interview more people in those jurisdictions. We are trying to understand the culture as much as the dynamics in those places.
- **Understand country dynamics** – Do a deep dive on those jurisdictions – external and internal politics, market dynamics, the role of organized crime, the inter-relationships of neighbouring countries, the technologies in play, the internal business leaders, and external companies (and countries) building out the economy etc.

[100] 'Around 2.5 billion more people will be living in cities by 2050, projects new UN report', 2018, United Nations / UN News

- **Set and setting** – If possible, go to the places and do the work in situ. Immerse ourselves in the culture and engage with the people in normal life and in business as well. If we want to know, then we must go.
- **Test ideas with people in those places** – Once we have developed scenarios, test them with people in those places. Then refine and test again. The people should include strategic partners, local employees, customers, government officials and others so that we gain broad perspectives.

Ultimately, we are trying to avoid a pattern of organizations expansion we have seen in the past – colonization. This is a heavily discussed topic in the foresight world and there has been a great deal of work to ensure that inclusion and diversity is considered in modern, progressive organizations. Organization X can build solutions for North America based on this thinking and it's likely to resonate with countries with similar dynamics. However, we've lived in a world where companies developing technological solutions ask us to sign our lives away and bend to their processes and ways of working. This is not a modus operandi that we want to perpetuate in foresight research and futures design work. We want to transcend that into a world where we create the foundation of plurality, inclusion and equity.

The impetus for avoiding colonization is great, as states Renata Avila and Andrés Arauz in their Open Democracy article 'Decolonize our future':[101]

[101] Renata Avila and Andrés Arauz, 'Decolonise Our Future', 2020, openDemocracy

> 'We cannot postpone the design of a shared vision of our planetary future. And that cannot happen without dismantling the colonial structures of our present... We cannot lose sight of the structural transformations that are required.'

This is what we must aim for in the futures design work we undertake, and there is more thinking on the futures consciousness that we should be enabling in Chapter 9.

What next for Organization X?

So, this part of futures design is complete and Organization X wonders what to do with this information, and how to broaden their perspectives. There are several activities that companies need to consider:

- **Vision** – Revisit the company vision to include bolder ideas of the futures in relation to the biggest challenges we face.
- **Strategy** – Review internal strategic planning processes to understand where they fall short in providing guidance, and to integrate futures thinking within them.
- **Messaging** – Carefully formulate their view of our futures and develop a communications strategy and key messages platform for senior leadership, PR and marketing capabilities, investors and the public.
- **Foresight capabilities** – Establish formal foresight and futures design capabilities within their organizations.

There are also important steps that can be followed to build bigger stories of our futures – using speculative fiction and experiential futures and the ability for the team to draw a line back from the futures we imagine to the present day using backcasting to find strategic considerations that inform current plans for setting a foundation for our futures. Steps 8 and 9 can be found in chapter 8.

CHAPTER SEVEN

IGNITING IMAGINATION

Strategic foresight lays the foundation to tell stories and create experiences that help people see, feel and taste what our futures might become.

Every story I create, creates me. I write to create myself.

Octavia E. Butler

When it comes to considering our futures, we need to recognize the power of storytelling is the most potent. It's been strong in the realm of advertising and marketing, but not a core tenet for all functions of a business.

Over the past few years I've been collecting stories that I discover in the consulting and design work, and at events and speaking engagements I have undertaken. Stories – and experiences of those actors within – can help us uncover the hidden structural and emotional complexities of organizations and society.

It makes sense when thinking about it. A great work of fiction, a gripping film or a campfire tale draws us in and activates attention, empathy and intimacy. And when we experience a story, it arrests our senses and imprints deep memories in our brain. That is the power of speculative fiction and experiential futures.

When we come together to listen to a story, our brainwaves start to synchronize with those of the person telling us the story. And, if we read a narrative, then it activates brain regions involved in imagining a person's motives and perspective and deciphering what it means to the individual. That leads to greater comprehension and creative thought. Then the listener and the storyteller develop intimacy as the brainwave patterns, ignited from reading and listening to narratives, mirror those of the storyteller. The story and the storyteller are important parts of this, as is the setting in which we are told the story. The deeper the experience, the more visceral, emotional and deep the story seems to go.

Thinking of stories that move us beyond scenarios into imaginative realms affords us the opportunity to travel down the rabbit hole into more emotional and visceral explorations of our futures through fiction, filmmaking, the creation of media and art, the invitation to experience the feelings of our futures. Through engaging stories.

What is the business value of speculative fiction?

In the world of foresight, speculative fiction is the approach of writing fictional stories or creating visual elements that guide the viewer through extensions of the scenarios we've created, or elements within them, to tell a story. Moreover, these are typically an evolution of the scenarios we've developed. Speculative fiction can include design fiction – short-stories with designed solutions; longer-form fiction – books and whitepapers; poetry and other literary devices.

Beyond that are experiential futures that immerse us in the futures we imagine and frequently provide something we can touch, hear, walk through and/or interact with. Both can take people into supernatural and other imaginative realms that allow us to explore the futures we speculate might exist.

Within these areas we find many creative people who are encouraging organizations to step forward into more creative expressions of what they can become.

I feel that the value of storytelling and experience is sometimes marginalized in organizations and restricted to marketing and client testimonials. Some random blog posts, pithy quotes and occasional PR home runs framed as organizational success.

This is strange considering that story and the oral tradition is how we have connected with each other, built relationships and crafted empathy in our communities. The stories represent us and provide perspective into the journeys people undertake in their lives – meaning-making and sense-making. That's valuable and should be cherished.

What is the actual business value, and can we measure that? It's not so simple because it's less tangible than revenue generation or cost savings, although stories and speculative fiction can lead to the ability to create those over time. It's a slow burn.

Paul J. Zak – a Professor of economic sciences, psychology & management Director, at the Center for Neuroeconomics Studies at Claremont Graduate University – has discovered neurologic mechanisms that enable cooperation and trust, and has found that stories are therefore incredibly useful within organizations. He found that people are substantially more motivated by their organization's transcendent purpose (how it improves lives) than by its transactional purpose (how it sells goods and services).[102]

Psychologist Abraham Maslow thought that self-transcendence was defined more by peak experiences than our perceived need for self-actualization – the realization of our full potential. In his 1954 book *Motivation and Personality* Maslow defined peak experiences as:

[102] Paul J. Zak, 'Why Your Brain Loves Good Storytelling', 2014, *Harvard Business Review*

'Feelings of limitless horizons opening up to the vision, the feeling of being simultaneously more powerful and also more helpless than one ever was before, the feeling of great ecstasy and wonder and awe, the loss of placing in time and space with, finally, the conviction that something extremely important and valuable had happened, so that the subject is to some extent transformed and strengthened even in his daily life by such experiences.'

While people who perceive themselves as self-actualizers experience this, Maslow believed that peak experiences allowed us to transcend ourselves, and he worked to close the gap and align more closely with ideas beyond the individual-centric – predominantly Western – idea of self-actualization towards our ability to have transcendent experiences beyond the normal or physical level, as seen in many indigenous, shamanic and Eastern religions.

The act of telling transcendent stories is one of the most powerful ways that business leaders have available to build meaningful businesses and to inspire, influence and teach people within their organizations, their strategic partners, customers and the wider public.

Therefore, organizations can create powerful stories of our futures to create who they want to be. In adopting the idea of storytelling – and of speculative fiction / experiential futures – companies can achieve much to empower employees within them. I think there are four parts to consider.

1) **Create a safe space for risk-free exploration** – is it OK to think about our futures, or is speculation heresy in the eyes of people who need to see us make progress today on the myriad tasks we have already been given? It's clearly valuable to learn from our mistakes, and it's

also safer to learn from speculations of what might be – whether positive or dystopian. Our stories can be delivered free of judgement and expectation. When we are relaxed and consuming new ideas in the context of stories, we can be curious and wonder 'what if…' so much more.

2) **Elevate inspiration, reflection and contribution** – stories can be seen as a feedback loop. They inspire our thinking and stay with us as intellectual artefacts living rent-free in our heads. They help us wonder what we can be in those situations that are shared with us, reflect against our own experiences and lives, and create new neural pathways that lead to new thoughts and ideas. They feed into the larger system that considers our positive and dystopian futures. I personally believe good stories are motivational speeches that drive action.
3) **Influence people to do more** – stories can be wildly effective in influencing people to change their current attitudes and beliefs. They ultimately transform the knowledge base of the individual and encourage behavioural change – either consciously or subconsciously.
4) **Encourage connections and community** – when we weave stories together, we forge deep connections among people, and between those people and the ideas and scenarios presented within. Well-crafted stories convey the richness of culture, history and values that unite people. The commonalities we find in our communities, families and between us as friends and colleagues bind us together.

The form in which our stories are represented needs to go beyond the written word as well. Marshall McLuhan, the Canadian philosopher and narrative theorist, famously wrote back in 1964 that 'the medium is the message' – and this has been found to be neurologically true.

The story may be told in print or online, in videos or pictures, in editorials or advertising or social media. It doesn't matter; all are mediums that can generate oxytocin – the magical hormone and a neurotransmitter involved in childbirth and breast-feeding, and associated with empathy, compassion, trust, sexual activity and relationship-building.

Stories are, in a way, nurturing hugs from our chosen family and show the world the wonder with which we are creating ourselves, and the organizations we are creating.

Shaping our stories

When we chain hypothetical scenarios together to create a larger speculation of the futures laid out before us, then we can create a bigger story. Of course, we can stop the process with a chain of hypothetical scenarios and then move on to backcasting, strategic planning for today and risk assessment with a more serious and broader perspective. Futurists and foresight practitioners often feel that this exercise goes only part of the way, and we often recommend a larger exercise of speculative design, writing and filmmaking to make the idea of dystopia come alive.

Stories have always been powerful tools for us futurists because they create sentimentality in the mind of the person reading or experiencing the speculative future artefact by taking them on a Hero's Journey (Fig. 7.1).

Weaving stories by combining hypothetical scenarios with antagonists and protagonists ultimately engages and inspires people at a deeper level. To do this we apply the Hero's Journey, a concept popularized by Joseph Campbell in which the leading protagonist – or hero – is called to an adventure.[103]

[103] Source: Wikimedia, Public Domain

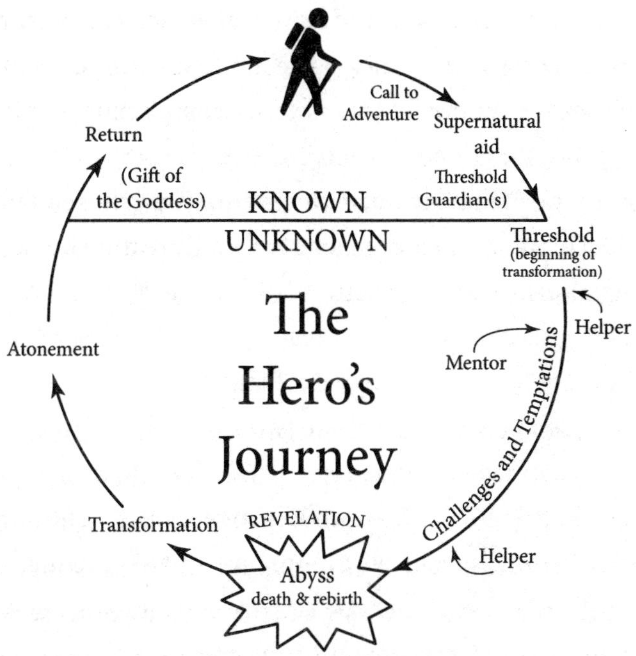

Fig 7.1 The 'Hero's Journey', or Monomyth

Along the way we can place helpers and guardians who assist the hero in the face of challenges and temptation. We can talk about what the *abyss* – the deepest part of the dystopia – looks and feels like. We can identify the actions and strategies that enable transformation from the dystopian state via atonement and a triumphant return.

There are some well-known examples of how the narrative form of the Hero's Journeys are applied in both literature and film with a view on future dystopian worlds.

In 1949, *Nineteen Eighty-Four* was released by George Orwell and showed us a future world of totalitarian control by Big Brother. It's seeped into popular culture (like many great stories) and we use it as a reference point to the modern panopticon of big data, social media, algorithmic control and surveillance. What is interesting here is that it doesn't go through the entire cycle, and the 'hero' Winston's story ends at Transformation and leaves an open end for the reader to imagine what comes next. I bring this up first because it's important to realize that we can apply this without completing the cycle. This is also a useful tool to encourage creative thought by the reader to extend more storytelling in the Nineteen Eighty-Four Universe.

Philip K. Dick's short story from 1956 – 'The Minority Report' – is another great example. Our hero is John Anderton, the creator and head of Precrime, a police agency that taps into the visions from three mutant humans called 'precogs' to foresee and halt future crimes before they are committed. The story plays with the idea that there are three simultaneous future time paths that all exist for the pre-criminals to follow. In the story, Anderton receives a report predicting that he will commit murder. He eventually proves his innocence, frees the 'precogs' and the ethically questionable program is disbanded.

Lastly, and one of my favourite visions of a future cyberpunk transhumanist future, is the comic book series *Transmetropolitan.* This was written by Warren Ellis and designed by Darick Robertson from 1997 to 2002, and showed a visceral dark future of journalism, political corruption, overpopulation, mass consumption, a myriad of multiple new religions and the emergence of a powerful force in what our hero Spider Jerusalem calls 'the new scum' – a derogatory description of citizens.

Through stories such as these, and the stories we will create, readers build empathy for the hero, guardians, helpers and other players in the story. They build strong emotional attachments to events, objects, places, eras and beliefs within. This use of connection and sentimentality heightens urgency for the reader.

An important thing to note here, and in relation to the Hero's Journey, is that an almost infinite number of stories can be created by mashing up story shapes in random chains across a book/film.

The Hero's Journey has been widely debated as being too limiting in its scope to provide a platform for every story out there. We need to remind ourselves that we are more complex and creative, and that our lives unfold in a non-linear way. We must recognize that the billions of stories underway at any one point in time interplay in a larger metaphysical sense.

The advantage of the Hero's Journey is that it does allow us to simplify everything into an easily consumable story – but we must remember that there are other ways to tell stories.

After a lengthy conversation on story shapes and finding alternatives with some foresight folk I found this fantastic resource: 'Beyond the Hero's Journey: Four innovative narrative models for digital story design',[104] which was written by narratologist Steve Seager, and which 'helps people design stronger narratives & become better storytellers.' He is critical of Campbell's monomyth because its aim – a Grand Unified Theory of storytelling to allow us to design stories that will connect with anyone, from any culture – is flawed.

Different cultures think differently about stories, which can greatly affect the perception of them and the events within. Seager explores four narrative models: Scandinavian narrative forms; Indian narrative forms; Central African narrative forms; and autochthonous narrative forms.

Scandinavian narrative forms – Scandinavian narrative forms are often built around multiple characters, with a ritual-based truth as the red thread.

[104] Steve Seager, 'Beyond the Hero's Journey: Four innovative narrative models for digital story design', 2015, *Medium*

Indian narrative forms – Indian narrative forms are radically different from Western forms as they explore complexity and non-linearity.

Central African narrative forms – these are based around a spiritual centre and rooted in physical and geographical environments.

Autochthonous narrative forms – The stories of the indigenous peoples of lands rather than the descendants of migrants or colonists. Seager generalizes a little too much here, 'these narratives are, in effect, all plot and no story. While the plot points are offered, the actual interpretation of the "story" is left entirely up to the reader.'

These offer us a bigger world of storytelling. If, however, we are to really understand what the forms represent and their potential, we must respectfully reach out to those narratologists, storytellers and knowledge holders within these four areas.

I want to dive into this a little more with Indian narrative forms. In early 2019 I found myself in New York City at the PRIMER Conference for foresight practitioners and folks working in design, speculative fiction and experiential futures. There I saw Pupul Bisht – a multidisciplinary foresight researcher and storyteller – give the talk 'Decolonizing our Future Through Inclusive Storytelling'.[105] It is described as follows: 'To address the glaring lack of non-Western methodologies in Foresight, Pupul developed a new futures method inspired by the oral folk-storytelling tradition of Kaavad from Rajasthan, India. Designed to support and celebrate a diversity of perspectives in futures work, this innovative method has shown to be effective in inspiring transformative visions of the future that

[105] Pupul Bisht, 'Decolonizing our Future Through Inclusive Storytelling', 2019, PRIMER Conference

reflect the authentic worldview of its participants. By engaging in a conversation about their unique histories and challenges of their immediate environment, this method encourages participants from historically marginalized communities to create visions of their preferred futures that reflect their distinct ideas of progress and are informed by their cultural ways of knowing, being and doing.'

The audience, and I, were enthralled. She had created a wonderful way to bring traditional storytelling and futures work together.

Living in Canada and connecting to the people here has been important but none more so than connecting to indigenous peoples. In 2018, when I arrived in Canada to live, I became great friends with Landon Gunn – a talented jeweller/carver of the Kwakwaka'wakw / Métis peoples – and Phil Gray – an artist/carver of the Ts'msyen (Tsimshian) people. The stories of their peoples and the traditions of art they followed were incredible. They were simple executions of scenes within bigger stories and representations of animal spirits.

We start to look for more autochthonous narratives around the world – from Australia to the United States to Japan and beyond. In doing so we can find an incredible world of variety and an utmost respect for the cyclical reverence for the natural world and for each other. We can also remind ourselves of the alternatives away from our industrial complex and its obsession with profit.

It is vitally important to remember all the differing possibilities and structures of stories when writing speculative fiction.

Exploring speculative fiction

In foresight work when we move beyond scenarios into wondering what if our world and the people in it worked and acted differently, we need to lean into speculative fiction as a first step to take those ideas further and to make them come to life.

I first came across the idea of speculative fiction via an interview by *Slate* magazine with notable cyberpunk author and progressive digital thinker Bruce Sterling:

> 'It's the deliberate use of diegetic prototypes to suspend disbelief about change. That's the best definition we've come up with. The important word there is diegetic. It means you're thinking very seriously about potential objects and services and trying to get people to concentrate on those rather than entire worlds or political trends or geopolitical strategies. It's not a kind of fiction. It's a kind of design. It tells worlds rather than stories.'

These words produced an instant shift in my thinking. The idea was powerful – and also frustrating because so few people were really doing that as part of the design process, and I was working in advertising where it was all product, all the time.

So, I went hunting for design fictions that felt more experiential. Sterling indicated that short films were a good medium for them and the first to catch my attention was 'Brad the Toaster'.[106] This was a graduate project by Simone Rebaudengo in collaboration with Haque Design+Research. Very simply put, 'It is the story of Brad, a toaster which is part of a new breed of products that love to be used. It shows the implications of agency of products in everyday life. What could happen if a product wants to be used?'

Brad is connected. Not just online but with other connected toasters like him. He knows what they are doing and how much they are being used. He gets upset if he's not getting enough action and will tell the owner he needs attention and use him, or else. After being

[106] Simone Rebaudengo, 'Addicted products: The story of Brad the Toaster', 2012

ignored for too long he'll ping a network of potential owners to find a new home and ship himself out.

It's a funny and interesting idea of how objects could be hyper-connected, eventually have intelligence and evolve to develop feelings. At the inception of the project Rebaudengo asked what if the smart objects of the future aren't just smart, but also potentially jealous, petty or vindictive? What if, connected to and benchmarked against their peers, their relationships with each other start to inform their relationships with us?

Rebaudengo did more than explore this idea via an animated short. He built a prototype toaster with sensors and an internet connection, and then made a further three to build a four-way Internet of Toasters (IoT – ha, take that tech futurists). He also built a website where we could apply to be a 'host' for one of the toasters. That's not just a story, it's a well-rounded prototype of a product experience. An experience where we wonder what our relationships might look like with the products being developed to have more connectivity and personality.

In 2013, Anthony Dunne and Fiona Raby released *Speculative Everything: Design, Fiction, and Social Dreaming*[107] – a book that: 'offers a tour through an emerging cultural landscape of design ideas, ideals and approaches. Dunne and Raby cite examples from their own design and teaching and from other projects from fine art, design, architecture, cinema, and photography. They also draw on futurology, political theory, the philosophy of technology, and literary fiction. They show us, for example, ideas for a solar kitchen restaurant; a flypaper robotic clock; a menstruation machine; a cloud-seeding truck; a phantom-limb sensation recorder; and devices for food foraging that use the tools of synthetic biology. Dunne and

[107] Anthony Dunne and Fiona Raby, *Speculative Everything*, 2013, MIT Press

Raby contend that if we speculate more – about everything – reality will become more malleable. The ideas freed by speculative design increase the odds of achieving desirable futures.'

For me, this was an invitation into a wider world, and into a new(er) kind of creativity. Indeed, the book is often held up as the beginning of the discipline of speculative fiction, and it certainly spawned a lot of work in the area. It gave people permission to blow the door of perception wide open through 'social dreaming'. That's a key idea that feeds into my thinking when I wonder: What if…

In 2016 a great friend reached out to me and asked if I had some ideas of how a futurist could help with the promotion of Vancouver International Airport's (YVR) Master Plan public consultation. Every 10 years they need to lay out plans for the next 20 years, and they looked for input from the people using the airport – the travellers and the surrounding communities – across six key areas: ground access, environment, community amenities, airside and airspace, terminals, and land use. The Master Plan was used to spark interest and excitement, YVR sought ways to inspire the public to be engaged, provide input and have their say in the future of the airport, and this was the second of four engagement phases.

I pitched my friend on the idea of using design fiction to ignite thinking and to inspire people what our futures could be like in relation to the airport – a place I had travelled from and to for over 20 years. I knew it so well; it's a quiet, beautiful place and held up internationally as one of the best airport experiences out there.

I sketched out the idea and he was on board. We prepared to pitch it to the client. They'd never thought of something like this, and they loved it – I think because they were open to the idea of storytelling more than anything else. Airports are the beginning, middle and ends for so many stories. (I have a secret – I often arrive early at airports and sit at the arrivals for a while watching what happens when people are reunited. I imagine their stories. It's always heartening. OK, let's move on...)

After the approval I went off to write five short pieces – 250 to 350 words – of traveller-centric and immersive stories:

Welcome to the Airport of the Future – a new arrival of a family embarking on a vacation and a new experience.

The Future of Personal Travel – a family leaves for a vacation and there's a surprise on the way.

The Future of Leisure Travel – a person heads out on an international trip to join a flight into space.

The Future of Business Travel – a businessperson arrives to find a transformed and technologically transformed experience.

The Future of Family Reunions – a child traveling alone arrives at the airport to meet family.

Each story puts people and their hopes front and centre. They then tell the story of the experience – the process and the integration of today's new, innovative technologies (which exist in early prototype and theorized stages) to help create a seamless and friction-free environment for the traveller – from entering the terminal to security to dining to landing to transferring and beyond. Here's the design fiction written to show us 'The Future of Leisure Travel':[108]

[108] Nikolas Badminton, 'YVR 2037: The Future of Leisure Travel', 2016, nikolasbadminton.com

YVR Airport: Thursday, May 14 2037 at 10:30

An autonomous electric vehicle with the Kakashi family onboard silently ascends the ramp leading up to the Departures level at Vancouver International Airport. Stopping in front of the Latin American airline entrance, the vehicle door slides open and two excited children bound out, followed closely by their mom, Deb.

Inside the vehicle, their dad, Yoshi, requests a receipt. A voice responds, 'Thirty-five credits for this trip, and we have you booked for a return journey for 16:50 hours on May 30th.'

Yoshi exits the vehicle and joins the others, while the vehicle glides down to the Arrivals level where its next scheduled pick-up awaits. The Kakashis enter a large, open-plan reception area adorned with First Nations art, framed by tall, glass ceilings.

Moments later, they place their bags on a conveyor belt. The bags activate an overhead screen, and a voice says: 'Good morning, Mr. Kakashi, your travel documents are in order and your plane is on time. You'll be leaving from Gate E127. Please proceed through the Security Zone and ensure that you and your family keep your heads raised for biometrics scanning.'

The family enters the Security Zone – a short passageway, walled on both sides with floor-to-ceiling, backlit panels. As they walk through, one by one, the panels switch from white to green, followed by a friendly voice that prompts them to proceed.

Once through security, they are greeted by the centrepiece of YVR's biodiversity and sustainability initiatives – a multi-storey tubular structure made of glass. Inside this tower, workers nurture and cultivate fruit, vegetables and plants, adjust atmospheric controls and gather produce for the day.

A holographic YVR Storyteller is on hand to explain: 'Welcome to our vertical farm. We use very little water in our hydroponic systems;

the water we do use is collected from rainfall and the power we use is harnessed from the sun, via transparent solar panel windows that surround the Departures area. To supplement the vertical farm's produce, we source fruit and vegetables from the finest growers here in the B.C.'s Lower Mainland.'

The aroma of deliciously cooked food greets them as they arrive in the airport's Shopping and Dining area. Travellers saunter from store to store, businesspeople congregate on moving walkways, and the international food court offers a scintillating selection of global cuisines. 'My friend Akio told me that the vegetarian café here is amazing. Let's go check it out!' says Deb.

While Yoshi and the kids find a place to sit, Deb selects suggested menu items from a screen, based on the family's personal travel profiles.

Moments later, a server robot arrives at the table with the food as ordered. 'Enjoy!' it cheerfully exclaims and scoots off to the next customer.

The kids tuck in and sample a little of everything. Deb and Yoshi exchange a warm glance. After eating, they make their way to their gate via the moving walkways and settle into their seats in the comfortable waiting area.

A boarding announcement is made and the family lines up to get on the plane. The airline staff greet them and check the family's credentials. 'Enjoy your trip, Mr and Mrs Kakashi. Jonny, Zina, we've left a surprise for you on your seats.'

They walk through the door and down the corridor to the aerobridge, the kids' beaming smiles wider than ever before as they continue their voyage of discovery.

We published the stories on YVR's Master Plan engagement website, produced an animated video short, and put billboards and sidings up around the airport. The President and CEO, Craig Richmond, and I then headed on a media tour locally with TV, radio and newspapers all connecting and discussing the possible future of the airport – to inspire the public to participate in meaningful engagement and encourage insightful feedback to help shape the future of YVR.

However, the most important part of this was the public consultation sessions. People from the local community signed up for several sessions and came to the airport. I gave a short five-minute presentation on possibilities and this was followed by two hours of roundtable brainstorming. My role was not to say: *Here's the 10 things to do* – it was to ask people to explore and think about the possibilities in our futures. That's an important distinction.

After the sessions had completed and with coverage from the media, there were calls from neighbouring cities to do more – which YVR embraced. More engagement is better. The results were astounding: increased connection with the surrounding community; millions of local media impressions, dozens of new, crowd-sourced ideas; and most recently, in 2021, the realization of an idea to present the Canadian west coast inside the terminal. The original idea was for a vertical farm that grew fruit and vegetables for use by restaurants in the airport. However, after feedback from the community, what was built was a 'glassed-in island forest with access to the outdoors' – a riff on the idea yet it's almost identical visually with immersive projections and whale song played as well. That's foresight and futures design at work.

Experiential futures

Dr Stuart Candy – the Director of Situation Lab, Associate Professor of Design at Carnegie Mellon University, and Fellow of The Long Now

Foundation – defines what experiential futures – often abbreviated to XF – are and can be:[109]

'An experiential scenario is a future brought to life. It's a tangible "what if", more textural than textual, and a way of thinking out loud, materially or performatively, or both. Seeking to collapse temporal distance and offset our habitual discounting of future events (Ainslie, 2001), XF angles for "what ifs" real enough to trick the body into taking them seriously. Its contours are generous, taking in "the gamut of approaches involving the design of situations and stuff from the future to catalyse insight and change" (Candy, 2015, p. 18). XF "involves designing and staging interventions that exploit the continuum of human experience, the full array of sensory and semiotic vectors, in order to enable a different and deeper engagement in thought and discussion about one or more futures, than has traditionally been possible through textual and statistical means of representing scenarios". (Candy, 2010, p. 3).'

I've already spoken about how the story, storyteller and setting are important. Now we have an opportunity to take each of those elements further. In traditional organizations we may see art, visionary quotations and company principles on the walls, ready for employees to observe and take to heart. Most likely they wander past them so often they become moot, and wall hangings at best.

So, this is a call for modern organizations to embrace deeper experiential futures within their spaces because it's these that will arrest the hearts and minds of employees. That is partly what my team

[109] Stuart Candy, 'Experiential Futures: A brief outline', 2018, *The Sceptical Futuryst*

and I aim to do, and we are finding more companies are bringing their C-suite, board members and senior executives along to learn how to do so.

Business games for futures exploration

In late 2018, I found myself visiting Niagara Falls to work with an energy company – a generator, broker and distributor of renewable electricity. The brief was to inspire them on the futures ahead in relation to our world and energy. Cool.

I suggested we could do more and proposed that the 280 employees in attendance play a game to help them imagine our futures – the 'Futures Ignition Exercises'.

Before the day began, I suggested that we take the 25 or so tables the attendees would sit at and give them names of new advances in technologies – machine learning, geothermal energy, automated electric vehicles, smart cities etc. I would then deliver a keynote for 45 minutes, followed by a question-and-answer session leading into two exercises – a brainstorm in groups of 10 and a futures headlines exercise.

The brainstorm was simple – identify the Top 3 disruptive influences that we think will impact our business and gain pace. For each, identify the opportunities for the organization that will come from these disruptors being commonplace by 2030. Employees had 40 minutes to work together (with me frantically running between the groups helping steer their conversations). They wrote out the influences and their impacts on the places and people they serve, and on the industry and organization.

Each group then wrote a newspaper headline from 2030 which outlines how the organization is world-changing: 'Wireless energy grid powers lunar colonies', 'Canadian GDP up 4 per cent due to renewable power innovations', and 'Poverty eradicated through dynamic power generation'.

Finally, each group came up to the stage and presented their work.

A couple of things happened in the exercise which are worthy of mention. Firstly, the employee working groups were egalitarian and democratic. The people's job roles were of no importance, and everyone felt they had a say. Secondly, the presentations were humorous and wildly creative. They had elevated their CEO to be a prolific superhero in some of the stories; in others they stated small changes with big impacts; and some were just outlandish and resulted in a lot of laughter. People spoke about the work throughout the day and into the evening event at a local vineyard.

Gameplay is so important in futures work and is deeply experiential. In fact, futures designers have developed games to help people think about the possible futures ahead of us.

Situation Lab – a collaboration coordinated by Jeff Watson from the University of Southern California and Stuart Candy produced a card game called 'The Thing From The Future'[110] which is an 'imagination game that challenges players to collaboratively and competitively describe objects from a range of alternative futures.'

The objective of the game is to come up with the most entertaining and thought-provoking descriptions of hypothetical future objects. One hundred and eight game cards are provided – of the type of Arc, Terrain, Object and Mood – along with some blank index cards and a pen for each player.

[110] Situation Lab, 'The Thing From The Future' – cards can be found online for download.

ARC cards describe different kinds of possible futures based on Dator's 4 Futures: growth, collapse, discipline, transform.

TERRAIN cards describe contexts, places and topic areas. In a completed prompt, the terrain card describes where – physically or conceptually – the thing from the future might be found – agriculture, class, climate, communications, family, drones etc. The creators included two terrains on each card to provide richer possibilities for the players.

OBJECT cards describe the basic form of the thing from the future: tube, snack, T-shirt, statue, tattoo etc.

MOOD cards describe emotions that the thing from the future might evoke in an observer from the present: delight, dread, hope, happiness, longing, sadness etc.

Several rounds of the game are played, and each player lays down a four-card hand – used as a creative prompt – containing one of each kind of card. Based on this play, players will imagine a thing from the future and discuss.

As the game progresses, players start to unravel ideas of our futures and what might exist within them. They outline the kind of future that the thing comes from, identify what part of society or culture it belongs to, describe the type of object that it is, and suggest an emotional reaction that it might spark in someone observing the thing from the present.

The player then writes short descriptions, reads them aloud and votes on which description they find the most interesting, provocative or funny. And, the winner of each round keeps the cards played for that round. The winner is whoever has the most cards at the end of the game. Simple. Provocative. Fun.

It caused much conversation in the futures community, and like all good ideas, it generated a lot more good ideas about using card decks to generate ideas and conversations of our futures. I also saw the potential for something like this to play a similar role in stimulating conversation around positive and dystopian futures and to be an extension of the work undertaken in the Positive-Dystopian Framework.

Creativity and storytelling in the foresight community

Events are great places for the foresight community to gather. One example is the aforementioned PRIMER Conference run by The Design Futures Initiative out of San Francisco. Their ongoing mission is to 'bring together designers, strategists, artists, scientists, and futurists to facilitate and advance responsible design and strategy practices that consider the ethical, cultural, environmental, political and economic challenges and opportunities of future products, services, and systems.'

I had travelled to New York City for the conference that year. In addition to great speakers on our futures, the process of foresight, and learnings from projects undertaken, there was a stream of creative work. The event was held at the Parsons School of Design and students had built an exhibit of experiential futures we could explore.

Design studio Parsons and Charlesworth were inspirational. They collaborate with galleries, biennales and other artists to explore the objects and habits of humankind. Their work aims to address key social, ecological and technological challenges of our time, including climate change and the future of work. They use sculpture, objects, narrative writing and photography to do so.

Being a great believer in transhumanism and Human 3.0, I was enamoured with their work – 'Catalog of the post human',[111] a project that they started in 2014 and extended in 2021 for the Venice Architecture Biennale.[112] In this they use 'objects as agents of change, the studio explores new typologies and prototypes alternate ways of living, often using narrative and speculation to propose scenarios that comment on contemporary issues.'

Second was the Nigerian-American artist Ayodamola Tanimowo Okunseinde, known more widely as ayo.[113] Okunseinde has created several interactive, performance-based works and performed in several countries, including Mexico, Finland and Croatia. He is also the co-founder and Director of Iyapo Repository, a resource library that exists to collect and preserve artefacts to ensure the history and legacy of people of African descent.

He presented his work 'The Rift: An Afronaut's Journey',[114] which 'wrestles with the misrepresentation of cultures and people of the African descent. The Rift holds that the lack of representation of these peoples and their culture in current projections of the future pose an existential threat. It argues that the denial of this "future space" distorts Africa's potential and denies the intrinsic human capacity of planning and organizing to its people. The effects of the above are an insidious erosion of the agency of the subject and their culture, and persistent alienation of their humanity.'

Both works were provocative and came from very different angles. What PRIMER did for me was open new horizons for speculative design and for the creation of experiential futures. It created an

---

[111] Parsons and Charlesworth, 'Catalog for the Posthuman', 2014

[112] Parsons and Charlesworth, 'Catalog for the Posthuman', 2021, Venice Architecture Biennale

[113] Ayodamola Tanimowo Okunseinde, 'Biography', 2020

[114] Ayodamola Tanimowo Okunseinde, 'Rift: An Afronaut's Journey', 2020

urge to see what people have been doing and to share their ideas with the organizations I work with and encourage them to engage with a wide variety of futures designers out there.

I collect numerous examples of futures thinking and speculative fiction work and try to share them with clients. Here are some of the most creative, funniest, challenging and thought-provoking experiential futures I have referenced over the past few years:

End of Life Care Machine by Dan K Chen – The End-of-Life Care Machine has been imagined to keep a person company and soothe them in their last moments of life. Chen sees a future where robots and technology can do more and more for us, and he wants us to start asking ourselves how far we'd be willing to let that go.

Mitigation of Shock by Superflux – Renowned designer Anab Jain and her team follow a pragmatic experiment in practising hope for a world future disrupted by climate change. The team built an entire future apartment situated in the context of climate change and the consequences for food security where people could step inside this family home and directly experience for themselves what the restrictions of this future might feel like.

Crisis in Zefra by Karl Schroeder[115] – Karl Schroeder was hired by the Canadian Army in 2005 to write a 'dramatized future military scenario'. The result was a book titled *Crisis in Zefra*, set in an imaginary African city-state around the year 2025 and focusing on the challenges a Canadian peacekeeping force might encounter when dealing with an insurgency in an urban war zone equipped with drones, cell phones and internet access.

---

[115] By Karl Schroeder, *Crisis in Zefra*, 2005, Department of National Defence

HYPER-REALITY by Keiichi Matsuda – This crowd-funded film presents Matsuda's provocative and kaleidoscopic vision of our future, where physical and virtual realities have merged, and the city is saturated in advertising, interactive games, and media. Technologies such as sensors, VR, augmented reality, wearables and the Internet of things are pointing to a world where technology will envelop every aspect of our lives. It will be the glue between every interaction and experience, offering amazing possibilities, while also controlling the way we understand the world. Hyper-Reality attempts to explore this exciting but dangerous trajectory.

Screen Surveillance Project by the Office of the Privacy Commissioner of Canada – The Office of the Privacy Commissioner of Canada funded the 'Screening Surveillance Project' – three short science fiction films about 'everyday issues around big data and surveillance'. They were produced to raise issues in our understandings of trust and surveillance:

'Blaxites' follows the story of a young woman whose celebratory social media post affects her access to vital medication, and highlights issues that arise when different data systems are connected.

'A Model Employee' examines data ownership and the need to earn trust within a formal system. For the main protagonist – an aspiring DJ – to keep her day job at a local restaurant she must wear a tracking wristband. She tries to fool the system as it tracked her whole life; however, a new device upgrade means trouble.

'Frames' explores the problems in trusting sensor data and facial recognition to interpret human behaviours. In the story, a hyperconnected smart city tracks and analyzes a woman walking through the city thus drawing what it sees as an accurate picture of the woman. Or maybe the smart city has it wrong?

There's one more experiential futures project that I feel really embraces the idea that we can (and should) consider our futures by looking at them through a dystopian lens. A beer company out of Fort Collins, Colorado – New Belgium Brewing Company – developed a beer in a future where climate change has had an impact on the brewing process and resulted in a 'beer not worth drinking'.[116] They developed Fat Tire's Torched Earth Ale by brewing it with smoke-tainted water, dandelions and drought-resistant grains. It costs $40 for two 16-oz. four-packs, and it 'tastes like sadness' according to Cody Reif – an R & D brewer with New Belgium.

They also commissioned Torched Earth's apocalyptic label art from Kelly Malka, a Los Angeles-based artist and first-generation Moroccan immigrant who 'has experienced firsthand the devastating direct impacts of climate change, including worsening wildfires and air pollution, in her own community. For inspiration, Malka drew on neo-futuristic worlds in popular films and television to depict the iconic Fat Tire bicycle in an uninhabitable world swirling with flames.'

I guess, if we are aiming to get the attention of the people (certainly those in the Western world), screw with their beer.

Building speculative design and experiential futures

I wanted to share several principles to consider when stepping forward to embrace speculative design and experiential futures:

- **Think about metaphors** – metaphors can humanize a story and imply a culture that has created turns of phrase, e.g. 'night owl', 'cold feet', 'early bird', 'couch potato', 'apple of my eye', and 'heart

[116] Keith Gribbins, 'New Belgium's Torched Earth Ale costs $40, tastes like sadness and is a preview of our climate apocalypse', 2021, *Craft Brewing Business*

of gold'. They are descriptive and inject richness with few words. William Gibson does well with the iconic opening line in his novel *Neuromancer*: 'The sky above the port was the color of television, tuned to a dead channel.'

- **Create unusual heroes, and many more villains** – We need to throw off the boundaries and visions of what heroes are and the tropes that continue their existence. Queer, less abled and low-income people have a place rather than a character like Batman and other rugged billionaires with unlimited resources. In modern literature we can find more diversity, but we need to go further. Look at our world and work out those exceptional heroes – and find the opposite dystopian-minded villains and make what they do and are capable of dastardly and motivated by greed and destruction. Also, be sure not to fall into the trap of over-stylizing these to create stereotypes that already exist.
- **Think about positive and dystopian situations and effects** – Positive futures are great, but the hidden systems are where bad actions and actors can exist. If we write scenarios and stories, work to consider the opposite of the outcomes. Then make them worse – more death, more despair, more impact on the people who are least able to react.
- **Consider what mundane systems surround our worlds and weave them into our stories** – Futures are not always realities of abundance and unlimited abilities (beware those futurists who talk about these). Think about the mundane systems, situations and job descriptions – waste management, water usage, newspapers, cleaners, accountants and even futurists.
- **Look back, reflect on the present story, and imagine what comes next** – Much like backcasting, we can try and see how to derive a path back to our present and understand how we got there – the

backstory. Also, look ahead. What does the story look like in 50 years? 100 years? 1000 years?

- **Try different narrative forms** – Move from a cyclical monomyth to an Indian shape or move to Norwegian folktales – transform. Whatever we choose, look to those practised in those areas and note their advice.
- **Diversity** – Always seek diverse perspectives. Never write a story in isolation from the rich tapestry of the world and without external opinion from those across the racial, gender, sexuality, nationality and age spectrums.
- **Speak the story out loud** – To people who will agree and, most importantly, to those who will not.
- **Draw images to represent the story** – Images and collages that provide abstract or detailed perspectives and views of the stories and actors within help inspire thoughts of the story.

For experiential futures, consider all the above and explore the following:

- **Build vs. Buy** – Building physical representations of our visions of futures from raw and recycled materials is powerful as reflection is built into the process. We can be in control of what is created entirely. It will take longer, though the results will be more impactful overall.
- **Embrace the senses** – What do things look like (vision), what do they sound like (auditory), how do they smell (olfactory), how do they taste (gustatory), and what do they feel like to the touch (tactile)? These make stories come to life – the orange tint to the sky, the smell of smoke and bacon, the dry, acerbic taste of vinegar, and the feeling of fur under my feet. Also, consider the less considered

senses of vestibular movement – the movement and balance sense, which gives us information about where our head and body are in space – and proprioception (body position) – the body awareness sense, which tells us where our body parts are relative to each other. It also gives us information about how much force to use, allowing us to do something like crack an egg while not crushing the egg in our hands.

- **Understand there are physical and mental spaces** – Work to understand the impact of physical abilities and mental / psychological effects within the experiences we design. Also, understand how our futures impact different groups of people and how their experiences affect each other.

Undertaking speculative design and building experiential futures is a wholly satisfying exercise; be prepared to put aside time for reflection and iteration. Once we have developed stories and experiences – written, visual or immersive – then we can really begin the work of exploring the futures that lie ahead of us. This chapter has aimed to shine a light on the process and some of the designers that have developed compelling explorations of our futures, I encourage people to look for more and notice them as we collectively dive deeper into foresight and futures design.

CHAPTER EIGHT

BACKCASTING

We explore our futures so that we can anticipate risks and strengthen the strategic thinking we are undertaking today.

We shall not cease from exploration, and the end of all our exploring will be to arrive where we started and know the place for the first time.

T. S. Eliot

The Futurist Think Tank and I have worked with many clients who find that backcasting is as important as foresight, which must feed back to action. Steps 1 through 8 of the Positive-Dystopian Framework allow us to explore signals, trends and well-considered scenarios and representations of our futures. While we could certainly undertake these activities from project to project and inspire people to consider our futures more deeply, we must also consider how we link those ideas back to where we are today.

Strategic planning capabilities within organizations are well-established and integrated at the deepest levels of the organization. Strategy drives progress, by laying out initiatives and roadmaps. That's not too dissimilar to futures work in its method – just more 'real' and with budgets, teams, products and customers who can be impacted in the short term.

The Positive-Dystopian Framework has two additional steps: (9) Backcasting, which then feeds into (10) Strategic Planning.

Step 9: Backcasting

Backcasting allows us to travel from the futures we have created back to where we are today by identifying cues and strategic considerations from the futures scenarios we have built. It asks us to consider what people need to be involved, what processes need to evolve or be installed, what governance – internal and external – is needed, and what solutions need to be put into place. It also outlines the programmes and projects that need to be established, and inspires thought about the investments needed and the individuals who will help support that journey.

Backcasting is particularly important when considering sustainability and is a tool to connect our futures scenarios to the present situation by means of participatory strategic processes that we typically find across the organization.

The term *Backcasting* was coined by John B. Robinson in his 1982 paper 'Energy backcasting: A proposed method of policy analysis'.[117] He presents backcasting as a tool to connect desirable long-term future scenarios – 50 years from today – to the present situation by means of a participatory process.

Extending that thinking, Karl H. Dreborg in his paper 'Essence of backcasting'[118] identified that backcasting is particularly useful when:

- The problem to be studied is complex.
- There is a need for major change.
- Dominant trends are part of the problem.

[117] John Bridger Robinson, 'Energy backcasting A proposed method of policy analysis', 1982, *Energy Policy*

[118] Karl H. Dreborg, 'Essence of Backcasting', 1996, *Futures*

- The problem to a great extent is a matter of externalities.
- The scope is wide enough and the time horizon long enough to leave considerable room for deliberate choice.

The main characteristic of the Backcasting approach is to involve stakeholders at an early stage in the foresight process and develop a longer-term vision of the desired scenario. Then all participants can translate this back into tangible actions – 'think in jumps, act in steps'.

Dreborg outlines the following steps to follow and I have added thoughts to them as well:

1) **Strategic problem orientation and definition** – Align with organizational problems to assess the present needs and clarify current and future unsustainable aspects. This step includes the identification of relevant stakeholders that can be consulted and can be champions for change.
2) **Development of future vision** – Create visions on how our futures can be established where the assessed organizational problems and unsustainable aspects are solved.
3) **Backcasting** – Set out alternative solutions and possible ways to develop our desired futures, and discuss these among the participants in the backcasting exercise. Also share these outside of the group and within key parts of the organization – this creates a larger view of the opportunity.
4) **Explore solutions / options and identify bottlenecks** – Further define and analyze the different pathways towards our futures – with solutions and organizational decisions needed – in preparation for the creation of action plans.
5) **Selection of option and implementation of action plan** – The pathways are discussed among the participating stakeholders and

one, or many, are chosen to be made operational. Part of this step is developing an action plan, including ways to tackle the bottlenecks identified. In the early stages of futures design as a discipline in the organizations. Attempt to do this with simpler areas first as it allows the process to be refined.

6) **Define roles of stakeholders and setup co-operation agreements** – A solid platform for action is set up, in which all major stakeholders participate. Responsibilities are set in long-term agreements and an innovation, or futures, champion is identified who can carry the work forward and build partnerships across the organization to make changes happen.
7) **Implementation** – The action plan is translated and implemented to the research and development agendas or the individual participating stakeholders. In addition, the organizational view is maintained and communicated widely – in an ideal world.

It's my feeling that backcasting should be undertaken only once time has passed since the initial futures work. Otherwise, it simply introduces criticism at the same moment that we are trying to communicate futures design work in the organization. That can limit our intentions and slow the whole process down, so we have found that pushing this activity back provides more time for deeper reflection versus a gut reaction to what people are reading for the first time. Of course, clients often want to jump in immediately, so the futures work must be protected at all costs and people reminded that the explorations are valid futures for consideration against current organizational goals and activities.

This is a reminder that futures design and its outputs can be challenging to accept because it looks at how our current state may change drastically and even become obsolete.

10. Strategic Planning

Beyond backcasting mixed with storytelling, we can more directly identify strategic considerations from our scenarios. If we scan all the opportunities and risks, we can start to identify several strategic considerations.

These should be considerations that can be fed into the strategic planning process today. This is the link from our futures to help anticipate roadblocks and risks while providing business value and foresight.

Steps 8 and 9: Backcasting and Strategic Planning – an example

At this stage we review the created scenarios, the opportunities and risks, the dynamics across Organizational, Cultural, Environmental and Technological factors. In addition, we discuss the following factors – Financial, Regulatory, Political and Social – and formulate a list of strategic considerations.

One good way I have found is to map it out into a high-level, intention-based roadmap from today and then (typically) through five-year incremental steps for four or five iterations: 2023 / 2028 / 2033 / 2038 etc.

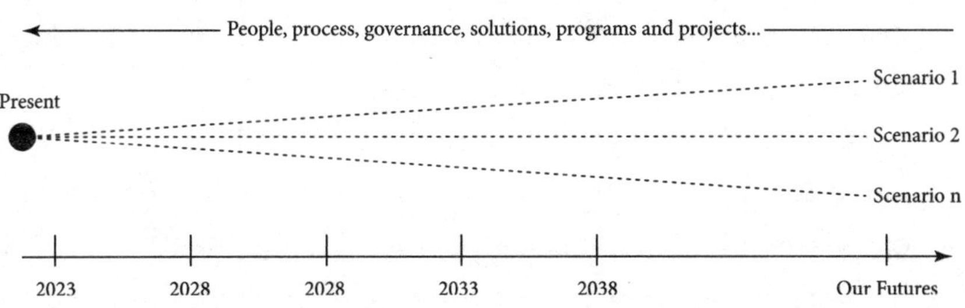

Fig 8.1 Backcasting Conceptual View

We can then consider our priorities, activities and factors within Financial, Regulatory, Political and Social dimensions, for example:

- **2023** – establish our visions of our futures and make strategic investments based on that long view with a clear understanding of business opportunities and risks. Operate in a cautious way to ensure that we can experiment and establish new companies, design capabilities, methods and intellectual property. Also, actively begin governmental relations globally in strategic destinations – North America, Africa, India and China – join discussions with the World Bank, World Economic Forum, Conference of Parties (COP) etc., and contribute to wider dialogues on our futures in the academic community.
- **2028** – announce new business models for community empowerment, launch new agri-food, agritech and media companies that will act as the foundational elements for Organization X's portfolio, establish new funds that support innovation in progressive food-energy-water systems and invest in new start-ups in North America, Africa, Europe and Asia.
- **2033** – grow our portfolio of water tech, agritech, renewable energy and new business models that support sustainable development goals and circular economic principles as agents of change from our current industrial complex. Our disruptive solutions challenge Old World companies that have underinvested in these areas.
- **2038** – while generating more than $1 trillion of revenues per year, we choose to invest all but that needed for running costs and dividends back into the systems areas where we have started to innovate. True transparency and equity is our

mantra and, while we do not expect people to always like what we undertake, we certainly aim to deliver good in the world every day.

Beyond backcasting mixed with storytelling, we can more directly identify strategic considerations from our scenarios and integrate them (this is Step 10: Strategic Planning). If we scan all the opportunities and risks, we can start to identify several strategic considerations.

For example:

- Understand the dynamics of grid energy providers and farmers, and how energy increasingly becomes a geopolitical tool.
- How to acquire arable farmland agrovoltaics while maintaining 80 per cent+ yields of food.
- Discuss how to stabilize food costs for urban-produced protein, greens and vegetables.
- Create a start-up roadmap and investment programme.
- Define community ownership models.
- Establish connections to government to develop new rules and regulations for urban food production.
- Architect solutions for reduced water usage while generating more food and energy.
- Understand that the staffing needed for complex technological farming systems requires new capabilities – data scientists, machine learning experts, cybersecurity experts, platform and machinery experts.

These should be considerations that can be fed into the strategic planning process today. This is the link from our futures to help anticipate roadblocks and risks while providing business value and foresight.

A WARNING – as a foresight practitioner, be careful to not be drawn too deeply into strategic planning activities. Organizations are best served by an outside view that maintains the integrity of the futures work. Remind people that futures work is speculative and directional and the strategic considerations must be further considered close to the strategic planning capability. Yes, there can be interactions between the teams but not integration of the two activities.

I want to include how backcasting can also intersect with other strategic planning tools within organizations – Brand Positioning, PESTLE and the Lean Canvas.

The intersection of backcasting with Brand Positioning

To create a strong brand platform, we must define the Brand, Product and Customer Truths. These, in turn, lead to a truthful and irrefutable positioning statement for an organization's brand.

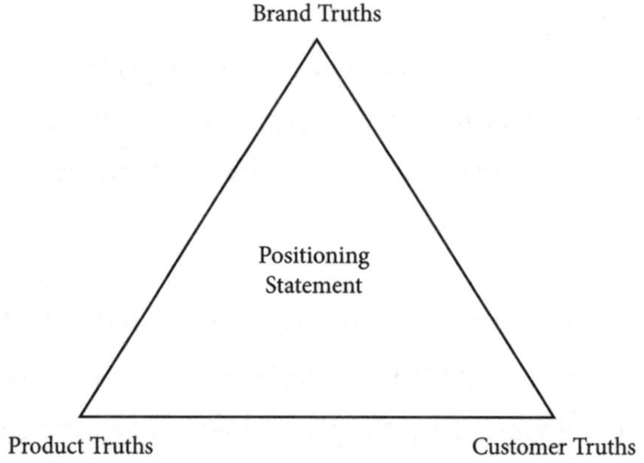

Fig 8.2 Brand / Product / Customer truths and Positioning

All of these will be defined in clear, simple business terms and will inform the creation of products / services, messaging, content and collateral. These also lead us to the creation of an organization's positioning statement.

Brand Truths – These are what the organization believes to be at their core – the essence of the brand. Is the organization really prepared for the futures we have designed or do we need to lay the groundwork today to reflect our futures vision?

Product Truths – These are higher-level functional truths about what the product is, and what it can develop to be in our futures reflected against our scenarios work. The speculative solutions play nicely against existing products and/or services in the overall organizational narrative.

Customer Truths – These are how the customers feel about engaging the organization to help with their performance, and their overall brand objectives as well. This is where we can take our futures design and influence our customers. How will our futures have a halo effect in the industry we play in, in related industries and in society at large?

Positioning Statement – At the intersection of these, we will see a transformation of how the organization considers themselves today but with the scenarios informing their position at futures horizons.

Some of the earliest futures design work I undertook came from collaborating on brand positioning with clients when developing messaging frameworks for marketing and advertising campaigns. It was logical to set our sights on futures horizons to ensure the brand was aspirational enough and ultimately *future proofed.*

The overall disciple of branding goes much deeper than I have touched on here, and the people in organizations responsible for the brand work, and agency partners should be included in the futures design activities.

The intersection of backcasting with PESTLE and Lean Canvas

Organizations of every size – from start-up to a trillion dollars plus in market valuation – use any number of strategic frameworks to help them frame the plans and roadmaps alongside product and service development. So, it's worth mentioning how futures design using the Positive-Dystopian Framework reflect in the workings of two strategic frameworks: PESTLE and the Lean Canvas.

The **PESTLE** analysis is a tool that is often used by organizations for situational analysis in complex and dynamic business environments. It helps them evaluate their position in relation to Political, Economic, Sociological, Technological, Legal and Environmental factors. While these can map nicely to the same dimensions we are using in FORCEPTS, they are focused on evaluating an organization's current state. The Positive-Dystopian Framework will deliver future-state views that can be valuable to consider in relation to the futureproofing of how the organization works and the products or services it offers today.

Political, economic, environmental and sociological futures – political dynamics on the water-energy-food nexus, population and urban centre growth, other megatrends, industry trends, and positive-dystopian factors affecting the political landscape over time.

Technological futures – the expected technological landscape we imagine might exist in our futures, the interdependent systems and how they operate in megacities and other urban environments.

Legal futures – this can be an interesting dimension to consider. What is the overall geopolitical landscape and how is that manifested in new legal frameworks and expectations?

What's valuable about considering futures against PESTLE is that it is a familiar tool within organizations. We can invite those familiar with this framework to also evaluate the futures work undertaken, thus adding more rigour and consideration. This leads to a deeper understanding and embedding of foresight as an omnipresent capability which will, in turn, lead to an organization with more foresight at its core.

Start-ups and innovation / R & D capabilities within organizations often use the **Lean Canvas** as a visual guide to help in communicating new business models and product/service ideas more effectively. In many cases it replaces the overly bureaucratic and verbose business plans. It's structured as follows:[119]

[119] Ash Maurya, 'Lean Canvas: nine business model building blocks', 2010. Lean Canvas is adapted from Business Model Canvas (www.businessmodelgeneration.com)

<table>
<tr><td rowspan="2">Problem

Top 3 problems</td><td>Solution

Top 3 features</td><td rowspan="2">Unique Value Proposition

Single, clear, compelling message that states why you are different and worth buying</td><td>Unfair Advantage

Can't be easily copied or bought</td><td rowspan="2">Customer Segments

Target customers</td></tr>
<tr><td>Key Metrics

Key activities you measure</td><td>Channels

Path to customers</td></tr>
<tr><td colspan="3">Cost Structure

Customer Acquisition Costs
Distribution Costs
Hosting
People, etc.</td><td colspan="2">Revenue Streams

Revenue Model
Life Time Value
Revenue
Gross Margin</td></tr>
</table>

PRODUCT MARKET

Fig 8.3 Lean Canvas: nine business model building blocks

The **Positive-Dystopian Framework** will provide us with signals, trends, scenarios and speculative products that can be reflected here. In fact, we can further elaborate on the Problem, Solution, Key Metrics and Unique Value Proposition (USP) parts of the canvas by understanding how we can reach the futures horizons that we lay out:

Problem – We can set out the key problems and related challenges we face today and state the future risks (dystopian futures) that will likely come to pass. Having a long view on this provides the ability to create a bigger and bolder vision of what can be achieved.

Solution – Our ideas can be reflected against the futures we propose. Are they still relevant in those futures? If not, why not? And how do we bridge the gap between the now and our futures?

Key Metrics – How will we measure effectiveness and performance in our futures? Our mindsets shift from revenue and profits to satisfaction and breaking even (after costs), and even to future metrics like life satisfaction, happiness and sustainability scores.

Unique Value Proposition (USP) – At the core of the proposition, what will make this a must-have product and/or service? With futures design we can further develop this idea and discuss how it provides value for customers today, in the near futures and for our futures horizons where we consider what individuals need.

Customers – The scenarios and speculative fiction / experiential futures can inform the organization on the evolution of the customer segments we are aiming to engage and how they interact with ecosystems at the horizons that lie ahead – modes of living, working, transportation and community through to support structures like governmental role and structure, and systems of support and healthcare.

Unfair advantage – This is the value of futures work. Being able to defend an unfair advantage – as it relates to the USP and other factors – in front of potential and existing investors is paramount. The futures design work gives well-considered and rigorous ideas of the complex futures horizons, and this can be valuable in telling the long-term story of the solution presented.

Channels – Channels are where we engage our customers. Today that is the website and articles, mobile application, newsletters, email, social media, online display ads, influencers, webinars, radio and TV.

In our futures that could be completely different with new modes of immersion and engagement. Having a futures view of channels allows for preparation and weaves in nicely to the overall narrative around the engagement ecosystem – social media, physical spaces, email etc. – we should prepare for.

Alongside any Lean Canvas, it's advisable to state the scenarios and futures design work that we have undertaken and which have been used as a reference. This helps bolster the case for funding. In addition, we may undertake futures design work once we have an initial understanding of our ideas and then take them on a journey into our futures.

Backcasting can be one of the most valuable parts of foresight work by enabling wider organizational acceptance of the futures design work undertaken. That acceptance is earned through collaboration, and we can build on the futures thinking we have established to include new thinking from across the organization. When this works well, it results in better futures design *and* improved thinking in core organizational capabilities.

CHAPTER NINE

FUTURES CONSCIOUSNESS

Exploring our futures and then reflecting on today's actions, informed by our hearts and powered by our compassion, will truly lead to positive futures.

The new truth is that we are one planet, we are one peoples of Earth, and we will live and die together forevermore.

It is now in our capacity to destroy civilization as we know it, or to build a world of unprecedented opportunity for all people.

Barbara Marx Hubbard

What can futures consciousness – a state of always considering our futures – look like on a personal and organization level? How can we bring together the ideas presented in this book and establish them as an overall way of thinking about the futures that lie ahead for organizations?

Consciousness is the human state of being aware of and responsive to our surroundings and the people with whom we interact. With regard to futures design / foresight within organizational settings it also means that we are driven and have a purpose to best serve people, planet and profit – the triple bottom line.

There are three things we need to create a futures design / foresight capability within the organization which supports the idea of both futures literacy and futures consciousness: executive leadership support; the capability to do the work; and, transparency in our processes and visibility of that internally and out into the wider world.

The need for Chief Futurists

There have been discussions in the foresight community on whether we should start expecting Chief Futurists (CF) to be established in organizations. Outside of that community there are strong opinions on whether it should fall under the remit of the CEO, COO, CIO, CMO or other established roles.

Foresight needs to be seen as a core organizational capability rather than a side-of-the-table job for someone distracted by other work unrelated to foresight and futures design. It is also not something we should aim to undertake as an occasional activity or hand over to a temporary team – no matter how good they are. It's a valuable discipline that can result in better strategic planning and communications today. This has often been the problem with innovation as a task within organizations. The value is misunderstood and sidelined.

This is something I discussed on the Exponential Minds Podcast with Dr Jake Sotiriadis. He was part of the initiative to establish foresight as a capability in the United States Air Force (USAF) and is also the Director of the Center for Futures Intelligence and Director of Operations/Engagement for National Intelligence University's Intel, Research, Education, and Solutions (IRES) Laboratory:

> 'We want to democratize futures more because we need to have more folks, especially in corporate boardrooms, and I'm convinced that one of the things we're going to see in the future, we're going to see a lot more chief futurist positions in the C suite, right. I have this conversation a lot with many companies and individuals. Organizations are starting to see the positive impact and value, they see that we want to have folks that understand how to do this, we want to be able to go and every company

now is recognizing, like, we need to have not only just a plan B and C, but we need to have a plan F. We need to really think carefully about, you know, how all of these issues, not just in our core area of expertise, but the things that we're uncomfortable with, how are those going to come back and then affect our bottom line?'

Organizations need a senior executive who is the arbiter of futures discussions within the organization and who works at the board level to influence company direction, determining decisions and engaging external expertise to supercharge thinking within the organization.

Maybe foresight practitioners have an opportunity to inspire leadership in organizations where foresight and futures design capabilities hold significant value and are a critical part of how the organization thinks and plans their way forward?

The question that organizations ask is: Where do futures design / foresight initiatives live?

It's not immediately apparent. Over the past three or four years I have worked with chief executives, VPs, directors and team leaders within organizations, and with external marketing, advertising and Public Relations (PR) agencies – and more. Without a doubt the most effective activities, and those that then become core capabilities, are sponsored by the Chief Executive Officer (CEO), who is the key person to collaborate with to create a futures mindset. Very rarely do we find CEOs who naturally gravitate towards futures work, though this is changing.

One client I worked with engaged my team to produce a research report, offer training on the basics of foresight and lead a workshop where the CEO, third-generation company founders and the executive engaged with the Positive-Dystopian Framework. The most passionate person in the discussions and exercises was the CEO. She had the energy and drive to continue the work and to establish foresight as a capability in their organization – and my team and I continue to advise them as they establish this.

So, now is the time to establish Chief Futurists in organizations. Organizations must step up to avoid being disrupted and their relevance in the market being eaten away as they hit their limits and potentially fall into a slow trajectory of collapse. A short-term vision just does not deliver.

I can see the value of Chief Futurists developing foresight / futures design capabilities that are well-funded and sponsored by the CEO and Board of Directors. I do think that this will be a high-pressure role – it may often be difficult to set out speculations before the shareholders, which makes it important to have solid data behind the speculative futures work. This will also be a role that is scrutinized and dismissed in the short term, at least until its value is more widely recognized.

Establishing organizational foresight

Chief Futurists will have the ear of the other Chief Executives and provide the service of exploring organizational futures. They will be supported by creative directors, futures design / foresight teams, signals analysts and external talent (subject matter experts, think tanks). They would be responsible for having a broad view on the global megatrends, signals of changes (relating to the organization's specific industry and others that will have macro and micro effects), developing futures scenarios, executing speculative and experiential futures initiatives.

They would ensure that they are in constant contact and coordination with the CSO, CMO and their ultimate champion, the CEO.

What does the Chief Futurist's team look like? Who are the players and what activities do they undertake? How do they support the organizations from a strategic and governance perspective?

As discussed in Chapter 1: What is Foresight?, there are six steps of the work the team will have to do: signal scanning; trend identification; scenario building; creating speculative fiction and experiential futures; linking out futures to our world today through backcasting; and sense-making. Organizations with excellent foresight capabilities are in a constant state of research, inquiry and discovery cycling through these six steps.

To create this foresight excellence, several new roles are needed:

- **Chief Futurists (CF)** – This is the individual who has overall accountability for futures work. Ideally, an experienced strategic thinker, researcher and foresight practitioner. Someone who has developed projects that explore speculative and experiential futures with a longer view – 20+ years. Someone who has experience of delivering large strategic and creative programmes. Someone as comfortable on stage, in earnings calls, and in the lab with the team pushing futures thinking.
- **Futures Creative Director (FCD)** – This is the individual who has overall responsibility for the delivery of inspiring futures design / foresight work, and reports to the Chief Futurist. An experienced creative director and designer with experience in product development, service design, writing speculative fiction, creating experiential futures, and creating employee and consumer engagement programmes. The creative leader in the room for workshops, creative review meetings and team discussions.
- **Futures Design Leads (FDL)** – These are the individuals leading the charge for specific projects, and reporting to the Futures Creative

Director. These are experienced futures designers and foresight practitioners with many years of experience in both foresight and strategic planning projects. These are the creative ideas generators in the room for workshops, creative review meetings and team discussions. They work with all parts of the organization's futures design / foresight capability.

- **Content Creators** – These are the individuals – employees, contractors and agencies – who are expert storytellers. They include authors, filmmakers, artists and sculptors. They work collaboratively with both the Futures Design Leads and Futures Creative Director.
- **Signals and Trends Analysts** – These are the individuals with an adept ability to be constantly scanning for signals of change and adding to an existing knowledgebase of signals and trends. They constantly consider the linkages and changes of hypotheses and possibilities for future trends. These are the foot soldiers of foresight in the capability – they are involved in projects, special initiatives and daily requests within the Futures Design / Foresight Capability and organization, typically coordinated by the Futures Creative Director.

I also think that it's a good idea to establish a couple of other initiatives: an Organizational Futures Think Tank and an 'artists in residence' programme.

- **Organizational Futures Think Tank** – Simply stated, a think tank is a group of interdisciplinary thinkers – scholars, designers, customers, partners and people that take an active part in developing communities – who undertake research around particular policies, issues or ideas. They convene to discuss these items regularly –

quarterly or half-yearly at least – and the output from these discussions informs the thinking within the organization, and the work in the Futures Design / Foresight Capability itself. Experts will cover a broad remit of social / public / economic policy, political movements, ideas and strategy, cultural change and technological advances. Typically, the Chief Strategy Officer, Chief Futurist and the Futures Creative Director are a part of this supported by the Futures Design / Foresight Capability to set the agenda for the discussions.

- **Artists in residence** – These are diverse artists and creators invited to sit within the organization for a period – typically one to three months – and create thought-provoking experiences and art pieces. They are not there necessarily to align to the organization's agenda or strategy. They are there to create a portal into a wider world. However, what they create is informed by the people in the organization and the work they see. They are also informed by the work that the Futures Design / Foresight Capability undertakes. This supports cultural and artistic exchanges, nurtures experimentation and new ideas, and supports research and the development of new perspectives and work in the organization.

Governance, visibility and transparency

With clear roles, accountabilities and responsibilities outlined, we set a foundation for the work. Programmes are created and projects undertaken. Beyond that there is the important role of futures design / foresight in the overall operations of the company and its communications with shareholders, analysts and the markets.

I was working with a large financial regulator and was speaking about strategic foresight and how it informs the organization. Within this I spoke a little about what Elon Musk had been doing – speculating about the futures for Neuralink and Tesla.

In 2020, Musk ran a press junket with several pigs implanted with early versions of the chips and the machine to implant them. They introduced us to a pig called Gertrude with a coin-sized computer chip implanted in her brain to demonstrate ambitious plans for a working brain-to-machine interface. Alongside this were relatively wild claims on futures where these chips could be used to help cure a long list of conditions, such as dementia, Parkinson's disease and spinal cord injuries. Big claims, and they were rooted in speculative futures. Speculative fiction informing internal thinking and the markets.

On 19 August 2021, Musk hosted Tesla's AI Day[120] where we saw demos of autonomous car features, a new AI chip for data centres, and a supercomputing system called Dojo. After the main items of progress were discussed, Musk announced he was working on a Tesla Bot and showed us what it would look like. The robot stood next to him as he discussed its future capabilities. Then we saw it move, walk up on stage and dance to high-energy music – but it was a dancer in a costume, not a robot. Musk insisted: 'The robot will be real, we'll probably have a prototype sometime next year that basically looks like this.'

Many looked on with disbelief, but I was excited to see this. A CEO of one of the biggest companies in the world, pushing boundaries and using experiential futures to show us how the future he sees will work.

Futures Consciousness

Organizational capabilities, as discussed in this chapter, are one thing, but the idea of an overarching futures consciousness needs to be considered. If encouraged, established and supported, it becomes

[120] Tesla, 'Tesla AI Day', 2021, broadcast on YouTube

an ongoing scanning capability that comes from every employee. There has been some great work undertaken on this idea.

In 'Future Consciousness: The Path to Purposeful Evolution – An Introduction'[121] Thomas Lombardo defines future consciousness as 'the total integrative set of psychological abilities, processes, and experiences humans use in understanding and dealing with the Future' and provides a list of the character, and organizational, virtues enabled by heightened future consciousness:

- **Self-awareness, self-control and self-responsibility** – an empowered personal narrative.
- **Realistic idealism** – the belief in and pursuit of excellence.
- **Self-growth** – a progressive personal narrative.
- **The skill and love of learning** – including honesty, wonder, curiosity, humility, and the quest for truth and understanding.
- **The skill and love of thinking and multiple modes of understanding** – including self-reflectivity, intuition and insight, and the virtues of critical thinking.
- **Expansive temporal consciousness** – a rich and thoughtful integration of history and the future – imaginative and visionary foresight – an evolved grand narrative.
- **Cosmic consciousness** – including awe, ecological and global consciousness, and a sense of reciprocity, justice and transcendence.
- **Hope, courage and optimism.**
- **Love** – including gratitude, passionate appreciation, and compassion.
- **Deep purpose and tenacity** – including discipline and commitment.

121 'Future Consciousness: The Path to Purposeful Evolution – An Introduction', 2016

- **Ethical pragmatism** – practical wisdom, knowledge, and ethics in action.
- **Creativity and the adventuresome spirit.**
- **Balance and temperance** – the integration of multiple values and virtues.

That's a lot to digest and to follow daily, but we can see that all these character traits and virtues come back to the idea that consciousness is the human state of being aware of and responsive to our surroundings. It is also often deeply emotional, something that organizations often suppress: work, we believe, needs to be taken seriously.

Lombardo's ideas, and the idea of futures consciousness, are further explored by Sanna Ahvenharju, Matti Minkkinen and Fanny Lalot in their 2018 paper 'The Five Dimensions of Futures Consciousness'.[122] These researchers outline three actor-centred dimensions that add some impetus to Lombardo's character traits and virtues:

'**Time perspective** – which allows the understanding of the past, present and future as well as the value of long-term thinking.

Agency beliefs – which depicts a person or organization's trust in their ability to influence future events.

Openness to alternatives – which enables critical questioning of established truths and seeing the possibilities that changes may bring about.'

[122] Sanna Ahvenharju, Matti Minkkinen and Fanny Lalot, 'The Five Dimensions of Futures Consciousness', 2018

In addition, there are two dimensions that focus on the larger societal level: systems perception – which helps to see the interconnectedness between human and natural systems as well as the complex consequences of decisions; and concern for others – which makes us strive for a better world for everyone.

So, awareness with consideration of time, the ecosystem of beliefs and influence, an openness to whatever is possible, paired with a heightened systems perception and concern for others. That can work incredibly well on a personal and an organizational level.

New modes for thinking about our futures

I formulated the Positive-Dystopian Framework to be practical and rooted in looking at all possible futures – good, potentially bad (dystopian) and everything in between. Over the past few years, we've seen some discussions about different ways to approach futures thinking. One has been discussed in some depth across the foresight community – the idea of constantly aiming to make positive progress towards our futures, or a state of protopia.

The idea of protopia was initially presented by Kevin Kelly on his website in an article called 'Protopia' (19 May 2011):[123]

> 'I think our destination is neither utopia nor dystopia nor status quo, but protopia. Protopia is a state that is better than today than yesterday, although it might be only a little better. Protopia is much much harder to visualize. Because a protopia contains as many new problems as new benefits, this complex interaction of working and broken is very hard to predict.'

[123] Kevin Kelly, 'Protopia', 2011, *The Technium*

This is the idea of our futures being a little closer, a little more real, and difficult to attain as we are stuck in the now with all the faults, risks and opportunities that almost stifle us in making plans to move forward to a better tomorrow. Kelly elaborates:

> 'No one wants to move to the future today. We are avoiding it. We don't have much desire for life one hundred years from now. Many dread it. That makes it hard to take the future seriously. So, we don't take a generational perspective. We're stuck in the short now.'

I wonder if protopian work is futures work in its purest sense. A nice term to attach to strategic planning that makes it feel more 'futurey'.

While I was writing this book, I spent some time in the high desert near to Joshua Tree National Park and managed to chat with Heather Vescent, another futurist, as I mentioned in chapter 5. She also considered the idea of the Protopian in May 2011, independently of Kelly, whose article she saw after posting her thoughts online, describing it as a needed 'positive portrayal of the future'.[124] Her perspective, in her own admission, was a little more radical than Kelly's:

> 'Protopians differ from utopias in that they deal with difficult problems without succumbing (and limiting themselves) to negative portrayals. Protopians are fundamentally a positive portrayal of the future with both style and substance. Protopians are both stories and people who think positively about the future. Problem solvers who don't shy from big problems, nor limit themselves to solving problems with existing tools, mindsets and paradigms.'

---

[124] Heather Vescent, 'Protopia Futures', 2011, heathervescent.com

This description references both the stories that will inspire the ideas of our futures and the people needed to make it happen.

The idea of protopias didn't initially catch fire in the foresight community, due to the potentiality of it leading to near futures work i.e. strategic planning activities. However, there is a progressive futurist that has been building a community of practice and thought in this area and has developed it beyond the original thinking of Kelly and Vescent.

In the past few years Monika Bielskyte explored these ideas and founded PROTOPIA FUTURES. This aims to 'explore new grounds of edutainment as a medium, bringing together the captivating power of entertainment productions, while also striving to deliver the value and the depth of educational endeavors.'

Bielskyte is working with a community of thinkers and artists on developing the platform to help create glimpses into radically hopeful futures, and to open conversations and explorations about what it takes to get there. She sees Protopia[125] as 'a continuous dialogue, more a verb than a noun, a process rather than a destination, never finite, always iterative, meant to be questioned, adjusted and expanded.' Her aim is for Protopian futuring to challenge the inevitability of imposed futures, and to not be solely bound to theory alone, but to connect ideas to a methodology that enables the creation of blueprints for action.

To be honest, I've been wrestling with whether I am fully on board with the ideas behind Protopian futures. I'm slowly coming around to it as complementary and a challenger mindset to established thinking in the foresight world. I look forward to seeing it in action within an organizational context where inclusion and diversity

---

[125] Monica Bielskyte, 'Protopia Futures (Framework)', 2021

should eventually stop being a tick-box exercise and become a modus operandi of operational excellence and progressive thinking that bleeds out into the wider world.

Protopian futures thinking has started to resonate in the design and futures community today, so do spend time digging deeper into these references and consider how we apply some of these principles alongside the development of our collective futures consciousness.

Ancestral and indigenous imperatives

This book is about designing futures and taking lessons from them, both positive and dystopian. In doing this work we are aiming to create better pathways forward for humanity. This is not a new idea, although the constant cacophony of the industrial complex makes it hard to remind ourselves of this fact.

In the preface I discussed where I grew up. However, I never mentioned the spiritual place that Wessex is: Stonehenge[126] is only forty miles away from where I grew up – a monument 5,000 years old, architecturally sophisticated and revered spiritually. Each year pagan rituals for the summer and winter solstices take place involving druids and people who respect the sacredness of our natural world. A place for hope of our near futures and reflection on what may come further down the line. It reminds me of the importance that paganism stresses on our deep reverence and considerations on the interconnectedness of all life. Those who follow that path work to live in harmony with nature. It's important that we come back to the view that our current environmental crisis and industrial complex exists as the result of humans considering themselves separate from and superior to the rest of life.

[126] English Heritage, 'Significance of Stonehenge', 2016

Much like futures design, 'paganism seeks to "re-enchant" the world and restore the sense of awe, wonder and magic.'[127] All of which we need to entertain in our foresight and futures design work. I hold that in mind every day and practise a deep connection to the idea that nature is sacred, and that the natural cycles of birth, growth and death observed in the world alongside an equally deep connection and utilization of progressive technologies will positively change the world.

When I moved to Canada and became friends and colleagues with various members of First Nations, I found parallels with that respect for the natural world, and it is something found in other indigenous populations as well. The idea of indigenous and local knowledge (ILK) has been embraced by many organizations trying to address the largest challenges of our day. Erik Gómez-Baggethun's paper 'Is there a future for indigenous and local knowledge?'[128] unpacks this:

> 'ILK is also recognized and integrated in the work of the United Nations Educational, Scientific and Cultural Organization (UNESCO 2000), the United Nations Millennium Development Goals (The Millennium Development Goals Report 2005), and the United Nations Environment Programme (UNEP 2007). ILK has also gained much attention from the Intergovernmental Panel on Climate Change (IPCC) and from the Intergovernmental Platform on Biodiversity and Ecosystem Services (IPBES), which acknowledges local and indigenous peoples as important contributors to the governance of biodiversity from local to global levels.'

---

[127] Denise Cush, 'Contemporary Paganism in the UK', 2019, British Library

[128] Erik Gómez-Baggethun, 'Is there a future for indigenous and local knowledge?', 2021, *The Journal of Peasant Studies*

Gómez-Baggethun goes on to say that 'Indigenous and peasant communities constitute a substantial portion of the world's population. In fact, the United Nations estimates that there are 370–500 million indigenous people in the world, spread across 90 countries, representing 5,000 different cultures. By the first decade of the twenty-first century, there were an estimated 1.5 billion smallholders, family farmers and indigenous people on about 350 million small farms. Altieri and Toledo contend that about 50 per cent of these peasants use local agroecosystems that contribute to food security at local, regional and national levels.'

Within these groups is a great capacity for adaptation and resilience in the face of so many modern challenges, from climate change to our society's cultural traditions. These people deserve our attention and ultimately they are active and important participants in our futures.

Indigenous communities have long operated with a view of thinking long-term. In fact, a prescient idea – Seventh Generation Principle[129] – is based on an ancient Haudenosaunee (Iroquois) philosophy that the decisions we make today in how our world is structured, built and operated should result in us having a sustainable world seven generations into the future. Around 525 years. This is often discussed within their communities in relation to many modern challenges. It is also a concept I have found to be alien in organizations.

These thoughts are included to encourage us to look outside of the doctrine of organizational strategy and psychology, business model canvases, and even formal methods of undertaking foresight. We constantly scan for wisdom from cultures and my keynotes often include references to ancient invention and indigenous knowledge. For example, I gave a presentation to the wood industry about the

---

[129] Indigenous Corporate Training Inc., 'What is the Seventh Generation Principle?', 2020

1000-year-old, vertical-axis windmills of ancient Persia that still grind flour and about how Hōryū-ji, an ancient Japanese temple built of wood in 607, is still standing and perfectly inspirational. We must remember that our ancient histories can usefully connect to our modern industries, and reconnecting people to what may be considered as simpler times and artisanal craft might just buck them out of the revenue-at-any-cost cycle towards planning for sustainability and longevity.

The designer, activist, academic and author Julia Watson has brought together an incredible book, *Lo-TEK. Design by Radical Indigenism.*[130] This is a fantastic reference that explores mountains, forests, desert and wetlands across 18 countries from Peru and the Philippines to Tanzania and Iran, to showcase millennia-old human ingenuity and 'a design movement building on indigenous philosophy and vernacular infrastructure to generate sustainable, resilient, nature-based technology.'

This is hidden knowledge but hidden only because many have chosen to ignore it. It's time to open our eyes and pay respect to ancient knowledge and bring that into our practices responsibly. And to teach important history lessons that can be applied in futures design.

By presenting this part of the chapter, I aim to recognize and pay respect to all indigenous peoples and those who actively follow paganism traditions in the face of more stifling and organized religions. I also recognize that much of the book was written in Toronto, Ontario, Canada – the traditional territory of many nations including the Mississaugas of the Credit, the Anishnabeg, the Chippewa, the Haudenosaunee and the Wendat peoples and is now

[130] Julia Watson, *Lo-TEK. Design by Radical Indigenism*, 2019, Taschen

home to many diverse First Nations, Inuit and Métis peoples – and in Palm Desert, California, USA – situated on Cahuilla territory with residence and protection of sacred lands by the Agua Caliente Band.

Facing Our Futures

Our journey into futures design and foresight has just begun and continues unabated. I hope that you feel informed and inspired by the ideas presented in this book and choose to take the long view and fight for our futures within your organization and beyond. I invite you to seek out many of the references I have mentioned within these pages and become actively involved in the foresight field, and look for the ever-evolving practices, practitioners and stories of the clients that embrace longer-term exploration of our futures.

We are never going to be short of challenging situations to grapple with and consider, and of positive possibilities for our futures. Remember, imagination is our superpower. Foresight harnesses that and makes it useful and applicable in our organizations, in government, across our communities and even in personal situations.

The one thing everyone on this planet has in common is that we are facing our futures, and choosing to do that together with an open heart and mind, and with a view to create an equitable and progressive world, is imperative.

Index

Note: page numbers in **bold** refer to diagrams, page numbers in *italics* refer to information contained in tables.

Index

Index